The Season for Getting Serious
GROWING INTIMACY WITH CHRIST IN ANY SEASON

ERICA D. HEARNS

THE SEASON FOR GETTING SERIOUS: GROWING INTIMACY WITH CHRIST IN ANY SEASON
Serious Season Press

©2016 by Erica D. Hearns
ISBN 13: 978-0990743026

Cover Design by Erica D. Hearns, Serious Season Press
Cover Image by Erica D. Hearns

Section separators designed by Freepik

All scripture quotations, unless otherwise indicated, are taken from the Holy Bible, King James Version (Public Domain)

Scripture quotations marked (NIV) are taken from the Holy Bible, New International Version®, NIV®. Copyright ©1973, 1978, 1984, 2011 by Biblica, Inc.™ Used by permission of Zondervan. All rights reserved worldwide. www.zondervan.com The "NIV" and "New International Version" are trademarks registered in the United States Patent and Trademark Office by Biblica, Inc.™

Scripture quotations marked (AMP) are taken from the Amplified Bible, Copyright © 1954, 1958, 1962, 1964, 1965, 1987 by The Lockman Foundation. Used by permission.

ALL RIGHTS RESERVED
No part of this publication may be reproduced, stored in a retrieval system, or transmitted, in any form or by any means—electronic, mechanical, photocopying, recording, or otherwise—without prior written permission.

For information regarding special discounts for bulk purchase, please contact Serious Season Press at inquiries@aseriousseason.com

For an interview, online magazine The Christian Girl asked me a question: "If you had the entirety of Christian women in front of you what would say to them?"

My answer is: This. All of this.[1]

---

[1] My actual answer, in case you were wondering what I think I'm saying in this book: Keep the cross before you, and let those things behind you stay behind. Don't stop running this race until you cross the finish line. Love each other enough to correct or rebuke one another. Don't let any woman who falls down remain down. Of all the labels that define who we are, Christian is the most important. Of all the relationships we have, our relationship with God is the most significant. Of all the jobs we may perform throughout our lives, seeking and saving the lost is the most rewarding.

This book is dedicated to my mother, Pearline Broyles. You have shown me in a million ways great and small how to find the good and persevere in any situation. The work ethic and determination you instilled in me and the unwavering support you have shown me have molded me into a woman who can grow wherever she is planted—just like you.

To my grandma, Rosa Mae Roberts, a woman whose strength, wisdom and insistence on showing gratitude have encouraged and challenged me to be a real lady. It wasn't always Walker Texas Ranger, Pepsi, and Peanuts; it was porch sitting, flower planting, thank you letters, and lots of loving advice. Thank you for loving us grands in a grand way.

I love you ladies.

Table of Contents

Acknowledgements	7
Author's Note	9
Is He Dead Yet?	19
Sowing Seeds: Study	27
The Ministry of Me	39
Ending the Empty Cup Ministry	53
On the Run	57
Glory to…Who?	73
Bare Branches & Barren Believers	83
Deaf, Dumb, & Blind	93
Taste & See	105
Just a Touch	111
Spiritual Alzheimer's	117
Bitter, Broken, But Blessed	129
A Woman in the Middle	143
The Ministry of "She"	151
Doubt vs. Faith	159

Discipleship, Mentorship, & Female Relationships	**169**
On a Mission, But Out of Position	**185**
Of Donkeys & Deliverance	**191**
Fruit or Flower?	**195**
The Miracle Worker	**199**
Success & the Serious Sister	**209**
Holding on to Your Harvest	**217**
Choose Life	**225**
About the Author	**227**

Acknowledgements

No book is written without the prayers and support of several people. God did a serious work in my heart during the course of writing this book. I will never be able to express my overwhelming gratitude to Him for trusting me to share these words with the women of His church. I can't thank Him enough for placing me in a community of women who love Him and each other.

I am forever indebted to Brother Maurice Blackmon and Sister Zelda Jones for allowing me to interview them for this book. The wisdom in your words has already produced fruit in my life, and I'm sure it will in the lives of others who read this book.

I would also like to thank my first readers who read and provided feedback on this book: my dad, Edward J. Hearns, and Desmond Alvies.

Special thanks to the Concord Street Church of Christ Ladies Prayer Breakfast ladies for praying for this book and supporting *Altered before the* Altar, as well as to The Women in God's Services (WINGS) ministry at the Fiske Boulevard Church of Christ for their support of my works as well as allowing me to road trip with them to and room with them at the National Ladies Lectureship. Sister Juanita Saintelian, my riding buddy and book promoter. Thank you for pushing me to promote my work across the brotherhood at ladies' days, conferences and lectureships. More importantly, thank you for your example. Your zeal in sharing God's word with the lost and your caring spirit are traits all young sisters need to cultivate.

To my church family, thank you for your support of me and this work: To my minister and his wife, Brother and Sister Harvey and Tonya Drummer, I owe a debt of gratitude for your support of my books and me as a person. Your wisdom and encouragement through this process has been indispensable. Special thanks to Sister Tonya Drummer and the ladies of the Westmoreland Drive Church of Christ for allowing me to speak and facilitate a workshop at our ladies day. Your encouragement and support mean the world to me. A special thanks to my elder, Brother Daryl Ammons, for lending me your copy of *The Strongest Strong's Exhaustive Concordance*. I promise you'll get it back...someday. ☺ To my Westmoreland Drive Church of Christ Church family, your prayers, encouragement to keep going, and anticipation of this book kept me writing many times when I wanted to quit. Your support of *Altered before the Altar* blew me away. But I'm most appreciative of the spiritual seeds you have sown in my life over the last nine years.

Finally, I would be remiss if I didn't thank everyone who has bought a copy of *Altered before the Altar, Altered before the Altar: Devotional Study Guide,* and *A Serious Prayer Journal.* The love and support you have shown for me and my writing has been far beyond what I would have imagined when I first pressed publish. I thank God for your hearts for Him and His word, and for trusting me to share some of what He's taught me with you.

Author's Note

15 I am the true vine, and my Father is the husbandman, ²Every branch in me that beareth not fruit he taketh away: and every branch that beareth fruit, he purgeth it, that it may bring forth more fruit. ³Now ye are clean through the word which I have spoken unto you. ⁴Abide in me, and I in you. As the branch cannot bear fruit of itself, except it abide in the vine; no more can ye, except ye abide in me. ⁵I am the vine, ye are the branches: He that abideth in me, and I in him, the same bringeth forth much fruit: for without me ye can do nothing. ⁶If a man abide not in me, he is cast forth as a branch, and is withered; and men gather them, and cast them into the fire, and they are burned. ⁷If ye abide in me, and my words abide in you, ye shall ask what ye will, and it shall be done unto you. ⁸Herein is my Father glorified, that ye bear much fruit; so shall ye be my disciples. John 15:1-8

There's something about starting something new that gets people excited. Whether it's a new job, a new relationship, a new year, or the first day of school, the nervousness and excitement of the moment is palpable. We can also experience dread and fear that this job, relationship, or year will end up like the last one, finding you in the same place but worse for wear.

Let's be honest: many of us have started a new thing determined to succeed only to fail. We've tried to do the same simple things a thousand different ways. Every year we tell ourselves things are going to be different. This is the time it's going to stick. I'm going to read my bible every single day this year. I'm going to lose 20 pounds. I'm going to eat healthy. I'm going to pray every day. I'm going to achieve my dreams. Nothing is going to stop me!

Except something does stop you. Life distracts you. People discourage you. Your free time and your available resources aren't what you anticipated. It's like the system is set up for you to fail.

You aren't alone. Here's a scary statistic: Forty-five percent of the population dares to make New Year's resolutions. Of this group, only eight percent are successful in their pursuit. There is an age old paradox being acted out here. Paul stated it best: For the good that I would I do not: but the evil which I would not, that I do (Rom. 7:19).

I learned a long time ago growth sucks. It's messy and hard. The discipline required is difficult to acquire. Making a habit second nature isn't second nature; it takes more work than you ever believed it would when you started. Maybe you wonder if you even have what it takes to do what you want to do.

If you've ever told yourself this was the season you were going to get serious about your Christianity and you're relationship with Christ only to fail, I'm right there with you. I've said I was going to read my bible and pray every day only to look up on Wednesday and realize I haven't done either since Sunday. I've set the goal to be in church every Sunday and ended up missing a week for an inconsequential reason. I've heard a convicting sermon and determined I was going to change my life, only for those good intentions to get drowned in the rushing waters and strong currents of everyday life. I knew it was important to cultivate a relationship with Christ, to grow in Him, but I couldn't seem to stay committed to the process.

Perhaps this isn't your testimony. Maybe you're like me in another season of my life. I went to church for both Sunday morning and evening services and attended Wednesday night bible study every week without fail. I read the bible before I went to bed each night and prayed each morning. I was involved up to my eyeballs in ministries. I made it a point to know everyone at church and showed myself to be friendly.

But deep down, I felt like I was missing it. I was doing everything I was supposed to do, but I didn't have the abundant life Christ promised. I felt worn out and tired, but duty bound to continue doing all the Christian things.

Hopefully, you don't feel this way, either. Prayerfully you are at a stage where you have a good life and a good relationship with Christ but you're ready to go deeper. You're still hungry for the word and doing the will of the Father. Perhaps you've acquired wisdom and you're ready to start sharing it by becoming more active in discipleship, mentoring or teaching.

Whichever scenario above describes you, one thing unites us: we are seeking to know Christ and make Christ known. We want more of Him and less of us. We want to experience all the sweetest promises of God held in trust for those who are obedient to Him. And we've decided now is the time to pursue more and greater in Him like never before. We realize checklists and standards of perfection aren't yielding the results we want, but we aren't about to compromise on God's standard. We are ready to do the hard work necessary to grow. Right now. In this season.

Who Needs to Get Serious?

The bible exhorts everyone, young, old, single, married, parent, child, or sibling, to be serious about God's word and being obedient to it.

- **Young people:** Remember now thy Creator in the days of thy youth, while the evil days come not, nor the years draw nigh when thou shalt say, I have no pleasure in them (Eccles. 12:1) This is an admonition to consider God and live for Him while you still have use of all your body parts and everything functions the way it's supposed to.
- **Singles:** The unmarried woman careth for the things of the Lord that she may be holy both in

body and in spirit (I Cor. 7:34b). Being single means having a singular focus on the things of the Lord. Learning who you are in Christ and being serious about your pursuit of His best for your life is your primary goal. You don't have to wait for a husband or anyone else to live for God.
- **Marrieds:** Wives, submit yourselves unto your own husbands, as unto the Lord (Eph. 5:22). As part of a married couple, you illustrate the relationship Christ has with the church to the world. The way you relate to your husband, the grace you give him, you do it all as unto the Lord. You can't be serious about your marriage without being serious about God.
- **Lovers:** Anyone who claims to love Christ has to be serious about pursuing His will for their lives and growing in Him. Christ said, If you love me, keep my commandments (John 14:15). If you claim to love Christ, you have to take your relationship with Him seriously.
- **Older Women:** The bible exhorts us to remain faithful unto death, that we may receive a crown of life (Rev. 2:10). Even if it results in death, we must remain faithful. We must finish the race that is set before us, running as one who wants to win (I Cor. 9:24). Older women are to be women above reproach who teach younger women how to do things in a way that's acceptable to God (Titus 2:3-5). They have to be serious about doing what God wants them to do to ensure God is not blasphemed.

At whatever point you find yourself on your Christian journey right now, you have to be serious about growing in Christ. As you read in John 15, any branch that doesn't bear fruit will be cut off and cast into the fire (v. 2). Don't run this Christian race lackadaisically; run to obtain your crown.

Why Do We Need to Be Serious?

Why do we need to be serious about Christ and who we are in Him right now? Our life depends on it.[2] Our eternal life depends on it. Hell is real and many are going to go there. Hebrews 10:26 states, "If we deliberately keep on sinning after we have received the knowledge of the truth, no sacrifice for sin is left but only a fearful expectation of judgment and of raging fire that will consume the enemies of God."

Even if you're a Christian, if you keep on sinning after you've been added to the body, you're still in trouble. We can't go to church, get wet, then live however we want for the rest of our lives. When you are laid out in front of the pulpit in your casket and the preacher says you gave your life to Christ at an early age, it is of no effect if you took your life back into your own hands somewhere along the way. You have nothing to look forward to but weeping and gnashing of teeth if you don't give your life to Christ for real.

Don't do what you know to do and hope for the best. Don't gamble with where you will spend eternity in this way. You're not picking lotto numbers. This isn't a game of chance where if you lose, all you really lost is a dollar; this is your soul.

God requires faithfulness and obedience from His children. We are called to do and be many things to show forth His glory to a lost and dying world. We are called to be a light to the world to show people Christ, as well as an example and teacher to those coming behind us.

We can't just say we are Christians; we have to live like it. Words won't be enough. Jesus said "Not everyone who says unto me Lord, Lord will enter into the kingdom of Heaven (Matt 7:21)."

At the same time, not everyone who claims to do

---

[2]An audience member answered the question I posed this way during a seminar I did, "Getting Serious About Who You are in Christ."

things in Jesus' name shall be saved:

> 22Many will say to me in that day Lord, Lord, have we not prophesied in thy name? and in thy name have cast out devils? and in thy name done many wonderful works? 23And then I will profess unto them, I never knew you: depart from me, ye that work iniquity (Matt 7:22-23).

Without faith it is impossible to please God (Heb. 11:6), but faith without works is dead (Jas. 2:17). We have to be obedient to the God we are so quick to say we believe in if we truly want to please Him.

We are called to teach, baptize and teach again (Matt 28:18-20), but we must ensure that after having saved others, we ourselves will not be a castaways (I Cor. 9:27). We must do good to all men, especially those of the household of faith (Gal 6:10), but we must not grow weary in our well-doing (Gal. 6:9). We have to be transformed and renew our minds every day (Rom 12:2) at the same time we're casting down thoughts and imaginations that aren't of God (II Cor. 10:5). We are to flee fornication (I Cor. 6:18) but to resist the devil (Jas. 4:7).

This brief recitation of some basic biblical truths can be overwhelming. How can we do all of this AND grow spiritually? How can I do all of this when I'm grieving, brokenhearted, feeling unproductive, unheard, or stuck in my life, constantly getting pulled off track by the busyness of life, trying and failing to conquer the same sin, or struggling to remain humble in the midst of amazing blessings and opportunities?

The heart of this book is to meet you in those difficult places and share what the Lord has to say in the hope it will strengthen and encourage you to pursue the perfect will of God and achieve growth in whatever season you find yourself in. Ecclesiastes 3:1 tells us there is a period of time for everything and a purpose for it. You are where you are right now for a reason. You ought to get out of this time the purpose God intended. And the purpose is always to grow.

In John 15, Jesus says God is the husbandman or vinedresser. God purges or prunes us so we can bear more fruit. This means every difficult situation is to grow you. Even if you ended up in difficult circumstances because you turned away from God, God can and will work all things together for your good if you return to Him, choose to love Him and pursue His purpose for your life (Rom. 8:28).

Being in Christ bears fruit. This means any good situation grows you. Connected to Christ, everything is for our growth and our good if we are operating in the will of God.

If your life seems overwhelming, perhaps it is because you aren't operating in Christ. Christ says in this same passage of scripture apart from me you can do nothing (John 15:4).

But I digress. We will get into the hard stuff in the forthcoming chapters. Right now, let's get you excited to jump into the thick of it. Let's motivate you to turn the page. You're going to get all the goodness God has for you on the other side of suffering! You are going to come forth as gold after you've been tried! You're going to bear fruit for the furthering of the kingdom!

Those are the goals. But why are we pursuing them? What does getting serious about who we are in Christ and experiencing growth in God look like? I need to know what this is going to look like so I can look forward to it.

What Getting Serious Looks Like

Getting serious about who we are in Christ, understanding who God is, and having a close, intimate relationship with Christ sounds good, but what does any of this mean? Pursuing God, His kingdom and His righteousness in our lives, letting Christ live in us and experiencing the fruit of the spirit that comes when we abide in Him has to have some benefits on this side of life. It does.

But before we get into what this looks like, let's dispel

some myths and settle some fears. Let me tell you first and foremost what this doesn't look like. It doesn't look like:

- A stuffy, condescending, unyielding law enforcer.
- A checklist or to do list of any kind.
- Striving for perfection and always falling short.
- Trying to be out front and getting everyone to recognize what a good Christian you are.
- Someone who does not suffer.
- Someone who complains and refuses to grow.
- Someone who chooses to stay small so they don't have to go to the new space God is trying to take them.
- Someone who chooses to stay small because they're afraid of how big they can really be in Christ.
- Someone so concerned with being big they can't be humble.
- Someone who can't be touched by the things happening to those around them.

What does being serious about God look like? It looks like:

- Christ--the life He led and the example He left.
- Imperfect people trying to follow in the footsteps of a perfect God. Failing miserably, apologizing often, repenting when they realize they're going the wrong way and going in a different direction.
- Finally allowing yourself to walk in the light, to let the light at your feet and on your path guide you instead of trying to outrun it or hide from it.
- Being able to be used.
- Being empty enough to be filled by God in a way far beyond what we can ask for, think or imagine.

- Life and life more abundant, packed to the full, and overflowing into the lives of others.
- Rest.
- Fun.

A serious Christian life is filled with hope, peace, joy, laughter, smiles, close relationships and friendships, fun, love, and service to others. It renews hearts and minds and alters our outlook on life. In short, it changes everything.

My Prayer

I pray this book opens your eyes to God's ways, opens your hands to surrender control of your life to the Father, and opens the house of your heart up to Jesus Christ a little bit more. I pray it helps you to fall in love with Christ all over again. I hope it drives you to fully appreciate the sacrifice He made for you.

I want it to encourage you to seek a more complete understanding of who you were created to be, what you were created to do and the relationships you were created to have in Christ Jesus.

I hope with my whole heart God uses my imperfect words to equip generations of Christian women to live for Him and show forth His glory to a world in need of Him before it's everlasting too late.

I'm striving to encourage us to be women with well-trimmed lamps whose lights won't go out before our Savior comes, women whose lights always shine in the darkness to lead others to Christ.

I'm praying being serious about God is something we become, not something we meant to do. I pray you're ready to commit to Christ like never before and experience the growth you say you want in Him. I pray you're ready to have a heart made of good ground. I pray you will be prepared to plant seeds of faith and reap the harvest of a more intimate relationship with Christ. I pray the yearning pressing you to turn the page and dive in is met by the Lord on these pages and transformed into a renewed spirit, a settled mind, and a heart knit closely together with that of our Lord and Savior's.

In Jesus' name,

Amen.

CHAPTER ONE

Is He Dead Yet?

> The reward is more than worth it. It's the getting through the mud and all of the sewage of that first step [that] is the hardest. When you're talking about coming out of the world...You come out but you have to take off at the same time. You're coming out of the world, meaning you're coming out of old relationships. You're coming out of old habits. You're coming out of old friends, old customs, and you're looking at a new way of life. But if you're not ready to change your world...it's going to be difficult for anyone to stay encouraged. ~Bro. Maurice Blackmon

I saw a news story once about a woman thought to be dead in Mexico. At her funeral, her family members said they could hear her screaming, clawing at and pounding on the lid of the casket, trying to get out. By the time they understood what was going on and opened the casket, she was dead.

Being buried alive is a common worst fear. There isn't much scarier than the thought people can think you're dead and bury you when you still have life in you. It's an instinctual, elemental component of our human nature to fight for our lives. Whether our fight is to run, physically attack, or freeze, it's a natural response. We fight when anything restricts our ability to breathe. We fight when our lives are threatened by violent attacks, physical or verbal. Our bodies fight against disease. As humans, we fight.

Yet being buried alive is sometimes what happens to the "old man" when we are baptized into Christ. When we are baptized, people are attending funeral services for the old man. Our old way of life has passed away. Christ is now alive in you, dwelling where the old man, the person you used to be, once dwelled. The old man was buried with Christ in baptism and is believed to be dead.

But what if he isn't dead? Can you imagine what the old man is thinking when he realizes he has been buried alive? As I said, our human, carnal, fleshly nature has an instinct for survival. It is not going to die peacefully. It's not going to be stoic and allow you to put it away nicely. It's going to fight for its life.

What is this new life supposed to look like? You may wonder how this life is supposed to be different from your old life. How can you stop being the person you've been all of your life? Conversely, you may wonder how you can hang on to the person you've always been. Everyone is insisting you should be a new creature, but you like the person you were. You don't like the sins you committed, but you believe you're a good person. You like your personality and enjoy the skills you were gifted with. You don't want to lose those good attributes of yourself. What does being made new really look like?

Anyone who has been a new convert can relate to the struggle of adjusting to this new life. It can be hard to wrap your head around the concept of Christ living in you.

No one can grow in Christ who doesn't understand the fight going on inside of them from the moment they are baptized into Christ.

When people get baptized, they think they have a clean slate to work on. In a way, this is correct. Your old sins have been washed away. But just because you aren't being held liable or accountable for those sins doesn't mean the habits, personality traits, and friends who facilitated those sins are gone. It doesn't mean the consequences of your sin are going to go away. You crucified the old man, but it doesn't mean he's going to stay dead. You buried the old man, but it doesn't mean he's going to stay buried.

> [I]t's hard to battle the devil when he got more help than you got. So when you're sitting there looking at your team and you have more demons on your team

than angels, you have to separate yourself, for one, or you're not going to survive that long. ~Bro. Maurice Blackmon

Most people, when they are baptized, come up out of the water feeling like a new creature. They feel prepared to walk in newness of life. They feel clean. There are people all around them who enfold them in this atmosphere of family. Everyone wants to know who they are, what their contact information is, and if they need a ride to bible study. They have a new community of people supporting them. They have a passion and zeal for God and His word. They never want to put their bible down. They want to pray and be close to God all the time. This is wonderful.

But then the service is over and everyone goes home. The new convert goes back to their house where their live-in boyfriend or girlfriend, children, parents or spouse is waiting for them. They come home to a computer filled with pornography or an iPhone filled with music degrading women, promoting lust, and glorifying lifestyles God opposes. They run into friends they used to smoke cigarettes with on breaks or indulge other bad habits with only a few days before.

This person may decide it's time to get serious about their relationship with Christ. They aren't going to play around with this anymore. There's no more halfway in and halfway out; they're committed to buckling down and living this thing. They throw out everything they own that's contrary to God: every CD, magazine and video. They block all their old friends and delete all their numbers. They grab hold to their bibles with big plans to read the word and fast every single day. They are grabbing hold to this Christianity thing with both hands.

But it's labor intensive and hard. They've gotten rid of all the evidence, but they still remember how to sin. Without thought, through muscle memory, their fingers can click through to the websites. Yeah, they deleted all the songs from their devices, but ITunes stores the songs in the iCloud; they can re-download them in a matter of minutes. It's easy to operate in sin on autopilot.

Their friends don't understand how they can look the same but want to be considered a new person. Their friends don't know how to relate to this new version of them, nor do they want to learn. Their friends want the person they were comfortable with back. The things their friends want to do don't relate to this new path they are on in life. Someone is going to have to change direction in order for them to continue to walk together. Who's it going to be?

The new convert goes back to a job they hate which doesn't pay them enough money, where they usually slack off whenever the boss isn't looking at them. But now they are a Christian. They're supposed to give more than eye service; they're supposed to work diligently as unto the Lord in this crappy, menial, below them job where people speak down to them and talk about them. Now they no longer fit in. They're one of "those people" who doesn't want to laugh at the raunchy jokes, share a cigarette in the parking lot, or go to happy hour after work.

Everyone in the new convert's life thinks she's judging them because judging is what "those Christian people" do. Family and friends see her as someone who points fingers and accuses others of being somehow inferior or less than. Everyone she knows seems to feel as if it's a duty of theirs to remind her of who she was before she decided to go "get wet."

Unfortunately, the people who seemed so excited to welcome this new person into the family of God become distracted by their own lives. Instead of keeping up with this babe in Christ, her new church family gets absorbed in their own issues or focuses their attention on the next new convert. Suddenly the individual finds herself without any support system at all.

She opens her bible hoping for some sort of encouragement and she reads Jesus saying

> 34Think not that I come to send peace on earth: I came not to send peace, but a sword. 35For I am come to set a man at variance against his father, and the daughter against her mother, and the daughter in law against

her mother in law. 36And a man's foes shall be they of his own household. Matt. 10:34-36

She reads "all that will live godly in Christ Jesus shall suffer persecution (2 Tim. 3:12)."

She feels like someone gave her a raw deal. What happened to naming it and claiming it, speaking things into existence, and walking into prosperity and her purpose? What happened to finally understanding why she was put on this earth? Where is the peace and unspeakable joy she was supposed to receive? She's wondering where she can get her refund because this isn't the Christianity she bought into when she came to Christ.

By making the decision to follow Jesus with her whole heart, she has attracted the attention of the devil. He is going to come for her. Hard. Whether she realizes it or not, she has been friends with the devil for a long time. He knows her favorite color, drink, what kind of guy she likes, and how to push every button on her console to get her to do what he wants her to do. She's done the wrong things so long it's become second nature. It feels natural. It doesn't feel like something she can change, and the devil will exploit this belief in any way he can.

The old man is knocking on the door of her heart again. If she'd just let him in, she'd have friends again. She would belong to a peer group again. She would experience some happiness, even if it was only temporary.

Everything within her is fighting against itself. It doesn't feel natural and therefore she must be doing it wrong. She's thinking "my sins were washed away; why do I still want to go back to them? I was told the old man was buried with Christ and Christ would live in me, but the old man keeps coming back and trying to move into my heart and control my body. It feels natural and comfortable to do what he's telling me to do and it doesn't feel natural or comfortable to do what the bible tells me to do."

Here's the thing, though: when the old man opens the door and walks in, he isn't going to be alone. Before, she could do what she wanted to do without being agitated or troubled by it. Now she can't. Now, not only does she sin, but she feels guilt, shame, and resentment. She struggles and fights with her carnal nature. She has a conscience now. Now everything she does has to be taken with such gravity. It's either one more step toward Heaven or one more step toward Hell. She wants to stay still for just a moment, to stop shifting. She wants the peace everyone promised her when she told them she believed in Jesus Christ.

She thinks to herself, "If I was really supposed to be saved and be a Christian, these Christian-y things would come easier. I wouldn't want to snap on people who mistreat me. I wouldn't still want to smoke a cigarette and have a beer. I wouldn't want to cheat on my spouse. I wouldn't have the urge to lie. Reading the bible would be fun. Learning about God, being close to Him and being in His presence would make me calm and virtuous. It would be like putting on a comfy sweater. But that's not what has happened. So I must be doing this Christianity thing wrong." The harder she tries to run toward God and work out her soul salvation, the more she gets knocked down. There's no way for her to be good at this, let alone perfect at it.

It may not seem like it, but this is the perfect place to be. The old man isn't dead until we realize God's place in our lives as the source of all good and perfect gifts. It's a continuous battle to keep the old man out. That old man wants to live. We have to crucify him daily. We need Christ to live in our heart if we want the old man to stay out.

There's no point going any further until we know if we've buried the ways of the flesh and are ready to live in the spirit. This doesn't mean we won't ever fall short or we won't struggle with any of the sins we used to live in. It doesn't mean we have to wait until we "get ourselves together" to get serious about Christ. It means we have to decide once and for all who we will serve (Josh. 24:15), whose will for our lives we will pursue, and who we will believe.

You need Christ to be new. Newness is God's gift. His

mercies are new every morning (Lam. 3:22-23). He makes all things new (Rev. 21:5). Christ's work on the cross allows us to put off the old man and the chains of our old lives of sin.

Good Ground Girl

The first step for anyone seeking to be serious about their relationship with Christ is to take an honest look at the state of their heart and evaluate if the old man is truly dead. Neither God, His Spirit, nor Jesus will dwell where sin is, so if the old man is still in residence in your heart, you are not positioned to have a relationship with Christ.

When we are baptized into Christ and buried with Him, the old man is cast out of our hearts. It is up to us to crucify our flesh daily, to deny ourselves and to follow Jesus. People who grow in Christ are rooted in Him and He is dwelling in their hearts. Clearing out the old man, the habits and people who populated your life, isn't enough to keep the ground of your heart weed free and fertile soil to grow a harvest for the Lord.

Look at what Jesus says about a man who has had an unclean spirit cast out of him:

> [24]When the unclean spirit is gone out of a man, he walketh through dry places, seeking rest; and finding none, he saith, I will return unto my house whence I came out. [25]And when he cometh, he findeth it swept and garnished. [26]Then goeth he, and taketh to him seven other spirits more wicked than himself; and they enter in and dwell there: and the last state of that man is worse than the first. Luke 11:24-26

In order to get rid of a habit, we have to replace it with something else. It's not enough to bury the old man and clean all of his stuff out of the house of your heart; you have to move Christ in. There has to be someone in residence so the old man can't move back in. In fact, if we only remove things from our heart without allowing Christ to dwell there richly, not only will the unclean spirit come back, he will bring seven worse spirits with him!

Many Christians today have trouble truly committing to the cause of Christ because they have let the old man move back in to their hearts and Christ has left. Christ isn't going to dwell where sin is. Sin separates us from God (Isa. 59:1-2). We need to abide in Christ and He has to abide in us if we are going to grow and have the life God wants to give us. We can't do the life altering, salvation securing work of faith if we aren't connected to the power source—Christ Jesus.

When you realize you can't be serious about your relationship with God or grow in Christ through your own power, you enter a place where God can work on your heart. This is where God pulls out all of the weeds and breaks up the stony soil of your heart so He can plant His word there and grow a crop glorifying Him. No true growth happens until we fully realize we need God.

CHAPTER TWO

Sowing Seeds: Study

4 Then was Jesus led up of the Spirit into the wilderness to be tempted of the devil. ² And when he had fasted forty days and forty nights, he was afterward hungry. ³And when the tempter came to him, he said, If thou be the Son of God, command that these stones be made bread. ⁴But he answered and said, It is written, Man shall not live by bread alone but by every word that proceedeth out of the mouth of God. Matt. 4:1-4

Many Christians know the above passage. The temptation of Jesus is a popular passage of scripture. But do we know where Jesus read "man shall not live by bread alone?"

These words were spoken to the children of Israel by Moses when they were preparing to leave the wilderness and enter the Promised Land after wandering for forty years (Deut. 8:3). It was one of the truths God wanted the children of Israel to learn in the wilderness. God wanted His people to learn to live by His word.

The same is true of God's chosen people today. The New Testament frequently compares God's word to food, whether it's the milk a babe desires (I Pet. 2:2) or the strong meat a more mature Christian should be able to handle (Heb. 5:12; I Cor. 3:1-3). Christ calls Himself the bread of life and says those who come to Him will never hunger (John 6:35). Christ proclaims those who hunger and thirst after righteousness are blessed because they will be filled (Matt 5:6). If God spends so much time comparing His word to food, it must be because it is essential to our health and growth.

I can't speak for you, but I need to eat more than two meals a week. I want to get more than enough to "tide me over"; I want to get full. I see no reason to ration food that's free and available in abundance. The miracle of God's word is like Jesus feeding the five thousand: we can eat our fill and still take up baskets and baskets of leftovers.

Christ said we live off every word that proceeds out of God's mouth. Why, when God has left a feast for us, are we starving? Why are our bodies (churches) malnourished? Why are we so thirsty when the word is described as living water?

We can't grow in Christ if we don't read the word because He is the word. He's the word that was with God in the beginning and was God (John 1:1). He's the way in which God speaks to us in these latter times (Heb. 1:2). Nearly every characteristic used to describe Jesus is used to describe the word of God. Aside from this truth, the word is essential for growth, according to Peter in I Pet. 2:2.

If you aren't going to eat the word of God, if you won't feed your spirit man more than a few bites off someone else's plate every week, you aren't going to grow. If we want to grow, we have to read the word of God daily. There's no way around it.

How do you view God's word? What's your attitude toward it? What do you use it for? Our answers to these questions shape how often we read the word, how we interpret it, and if we will apply it to our lives.

There are two distinct attitudes Christians take toward God's word worth exploring when discussing growth. Both can be found in scripture and reflect how our attitude and views on God's word can aid our growth or wither us faster.

While the children of Israel camped near Mt. Sinai, the voice of the Lord descended on the mountain. A thick cloud of smoke surrounded the mountaintop. His voice was like the sounds of trumpets and thunder. The people could not touch the mountain, but they could hear God. This display terrified them. They told Moses to go and talk to God because this voice was too terrible. While Moses is away receiving the law, the children of Israel build the golden calf and begin to worship it instead of God.

Psalms 1 describes a much different attitude to hearing from God. It says blessed is the man who delights in the law of the Lord and meditates in it day and night (Psalm 1:2). It goes on to describe this man as being like a tree planted by rivers of water. This tree brings forth fruit in his season and his leaves don't wither. Everything this man does prospers (v.3).

How do you respond to God's word? Is it the response of the children of Israel at Mount Sinai, or is it the response of Jesus in the wilderness? Are you terrified of the word or living off of it? Do you fear it or do you delight in it? Do you send others to go and bring back the word of God to you, or do you meditate in it day and night? The answers to these questions will directly correspond to the rate of your spiritual growth and development.

Many today, like the children of Israel, want to send someone else to speak to God, offer up sacrifices for their sins, and listen to God's voice. They want prophets to tell them what's going to happen. They want to go to church and sit under someone who has studied or heard from the Lord instead of hearing from God themselves.

Here's the thing those people are missing: the word of God is alive and active. It cuts to the thoughts and intents of the heart (Heb. 4:12). It is the seed God wants to plant in our hearts to grow a harvest for Him. We can't have faith if we don't hear the word of God (Rom 10:17). We can't build a relationship with Christ without learning about who He is, and we learn of Him through His word. The word of God is essential.

One of the inherent dangers of waiting for someone to bring back the word for you is while you're waiting for them to come back, your life is still moving forward. You're still in the midst of your life, dealing with struggles and hardships. You're still searching for answers. You're still doing whatever you can to survive.

In the course of our everyday lives, if we're waiting for Sunday or Wednesday for someone to bring us back a word from the Lord, all the distractions, setbacks, and weights of life will weigh us down. This can breed bitterness in us. We won't know why things are happening to us or what we should do about the challenges we face because we haven't read the word or heard from the Lord. This can lead to a loss of faith.

We need the word in us to combat the sin in the world around us. We have to feed the spirit man if we want him to be strong enough to resist the devil. The junk food of this world won't fill him or grow him; only God's word can do that.

The children of Israel were separated from God in ways we don't have to be. They had to go to the priest to offer sacrifices or for prayer. Prophets had to bring them word from the Lord. There was a veil between the holy place and the place where God's presence sat on the mercy seat in the Holy of Holies (Ex. 26:33-34, Lev. 16:2). The people weren't able to hear directly from Him or make their request known to Him in the same way we are free to do today. The ripping of the temple veil when Christ died on the cross was the end of the separation between God and His people (Matt. 27:51). Now we can come boldly before Him and make our requests known (Heb. 4:16). We can have a deeper relationship with Him. Now we can hear from God directly any time we want by opening our bibles.

We can't latch on to the privilege of prayer while we refuse the command to study. We can't claim an intimate relationship with Christ if we never learn of Him through the word. How do we claim Jesus as our Lord and Savior, brother and friend, when we won't take the time to learn who He is through His word? How many intimate relationships do you have where only one of you is interested in knowing and understanding the other?

What is the word? Why is it so important to be serious about studying the word?

- **The word is the way we learn of God.** It tells us who God is, what He has done, and

what He will do.
- **The word is how we govern ourselves and bring our lives into line with God's will.** All scripture is God-breathed. It is profitable, or useful, for instruction, rebuking, correcting and training in righteousness (II Tim. 3:16 NIV). In other words, the word not only provides instruction, but it can be used to convict us, correct us, and conform us to the will of God for His people. It's what we use to tell each other when we are doing wrong as well as what we use to encourage one another to do the right things. The word is the compass we should use to navigate through life.
- **The word is how we evaluate truth.** We are to study the word to show ourselves approved. We should be able to rightly divide the word of truth. The amplified version says "accurately handling and skillfully teaching the word of truth." What this means is we shouldn't cherry pick scriptures, quoting them out of context or twisting them to justify our stances or agendas. We should be able to understand what the scriptures really mean. When we listen to sermons or participate in Sunday school, we should search the scriptures to see if what is being preached and taught is correct according to the scriptures. God's word is the standard for truth.
- **The word of God is alive and active.** It is powerful. The bible says it's sharper than a two edged sword (Heb. 4:12). It penetrates us so deeply, it can divide our soul from our spirit and our joints from our marrow. It exposes and judges the thoughts and intents of the heart. In other words, God's word cuts to the deepest parts of our nature and the essence of who and what we are. Like a double edged sword, it cuts going in and coming out. All this

cutting isn't to harm us. The same way surgeons use sharp implements to cut out diseased or damaged parts, the word of God plucks out the parts of us sin has infected. This cutting away of a part is to save the whole. It profits us to learn to use the word to save and heal in this way. It's important for us to know what's hiding in the deepest parts of us, to expose it to the light of truth. God already knows what's inside of us; His word helps us to know as well.

- **The word of God is the food we need to survive.** It's a source of life, and it is life. Jesus said the words He speaks are Spirit and life (John 6:63). The word of God delivers us, develops us, and disciplines us. It's a gift from God. We should teach it as a privilege and not a penalty.

It's important to point out scripture is described as being God-breathed (NIV, AMP). Do you know what else is God breathed? God breathed into Adam the breath of life and man became a living soul (Gen. 2:7). God did not breathe into anything else He created. But He breathed into us and His word.

Our word has some power in it because of this. The bible says death and life are in the power of the tongue (Prov. 18:21). Our word is powerful. What we say changes things. But think how much more powerful God's word is, how much more life giving and sustaining.

God's word comes from Him. It has His hallmarks. It is holy, righteous, and perfect. What we say is influenced by what we've fed our hearts. Will it be blessing or cursing? Will it be death or life? You can't get out what you haven't put in. If things aren't living and growing around you, maybe you haven't been eating the word of life.

Some Christians view God's word as burdensome, boring, or difficult. They believe it's for someone else to interpret and bring back to them. It's something they only need a little bit of. They can get prayed up or "worded up" on Sundays and Wednesdays. This will be enough to sustain them. When we believe this, it's because we have quenched the Holy Spirit. We've put out the fire in us to do God's will. We've begun to satisfy ourselves through other pursuits. We're full from spiritual junk food. A little bit of bible takes care of our hunger and thirst. "I heard the word on Sunday. That's good enough. That's enough word. I'm straight. I don't need any more this week."

We do ourselves a disservice because we open ourselves up to false teachers and false preachers. People are led astray by false teachers and smooth talkers because they don't know the word for themselves. They're allowing other people to tell them what the word says and sometimes those people are not of God. Sometimes those people aren't telling them what the Word says. They're not rightly dividing scripture; instead, they're taking a scripture from here and one from there to justify whatever they want to do. People end up cosigning people who are leading them astray.

In the church today, people are asking for or accepting watered down rhyming slogans, alliterations and affirmations in place of the true word of Good. They want people to preach prosperity and the promises of God without proclaiming the punishment for disobedience and sinfulness. They are letting unbiblical practices creep in because they have not been paying attention. I like how in Acts the Bereans were searching the scriptures to see if what the apostles preached was in line with scripture (Acts 17:11). They weren't just taking their word for it, but they were studying.

Beyond making sure we are hearing from God, our spirit man is being fed and nourished, we are able to spot false teachers, preachers and "prophets" and what having the word in us means for us, we must be cognizant of what having the word in us means for other people. We're supposed to be prepared to give an answer for the faith in us. We're supposed to be able to speak in season and out of season at any time to anyone. We are supposed to teach people about Christ, baptize them and teach them again.

How can you teach somebody something you don't know? How can you explain something to somebody when it's only a feeling for you? What happens when your feelings change and you have no basis in the Word?

There are many being swayed from their faith by convincing arguments because they don't know the scriptures well enough to give an answer in season and out of season for what they believe. They don't even know what it is they're supposed to believe or what they're supposed to do. Jesus meets several people who don't know the word or who lean more on tradition than the word. He says several times "if you knew who it was that was speaking to you, you would have asked for this" or "if you knew who it was that was among you, you would have asked for this." We don't know what to ask God for because we don't know who He is. I'll say that again: We don't know what to ask God for because we don't know who He is. We limit what God can do and who God is by not reading His word to see what God has done, what He will do, what He is capable of, and what He is not capable of. We do ourselves a disservice.

The Declaration of Independence. The Gettysburg Address. The twenty-seven Amendments to the Constitution, particularly the first ten known as the Bill of Rights. The Order of Operations for mathematical equations. The Periodic Table of the Elements. Every President of the United States of America.

These are all things I used to know by heart. I studied them for hours. I made flash cards and learned mnemonic devices to remember them. My mother bought me placemats with the Presidents and maps of the United States with the state capitals labeled. I ate, slept, and breathed in each and every one of these things and knew them backwards and forwards.

I don't remember most of these things by heart anymore. I remember the general gist. I remember fourscore and something years ago, our forefathers did some things to bring about a great nation to do some stuff. According to Mental Floss quizzes, I can name more

Presidents than most of my friends on Facebook. I can't speak for you, but those hours of study and memory didn't profit me much. I got an "A" on the exam or felt a feeling of accomplishment for knowing it, then I promptly forgot it.

Sometimes we do the same thing with God's word. When we first became a Christian, or at some other point when we decided to become serious about seeking after the Lord, we decided to memorize scripture or really study the Bible. Maybe you learned a lot and passed some tests.

But somewhere along the way, maybe it became a party trick to be able to quote whole passages of scripture, or maybe you decided subconsciously since you passed the test, you could forget it and replace your knowledge of scripture with something else. Maybe your schedule got too busy or you chose to sleep in a few too many times, but somewhere along the way you didn't make it a priority.

Perhaps you weren't understanding the word. You could quote it but you didn't know what it meant. Maybe you started reading through the bible and got stuck in Leviticus (too many specific laws), Numbers (its interminable listings of people), Kings (those long descriptions of the temple can be brutal), Jeremiah (jumping around in time), or Revelations (too much symbolism). Maybe you really want to study God's word for yourself and be able to apply it to your life, but you don't know how. Like a baby, it's just easier to let someone else feed you.

Here's the thing: all of those examples I listed were things I memorized, not things I wrote on my heart. The bible teaches us to write God's word on our hearts (Ex. 13:9, Deut. 11:18, Prov. 3:3; 6:21; 7:3).

How do you do that? How do you apply it to your life? How do you make studying God's word or memorizing scripture more than a bunch of useless information taking up space in your head, soon to be flushed out when space is needed for something else? How do you let the word dwell in you richly and become an everlasting spring in you?

1. You have to know what the Bible (God's

word) is for—its purpose.
2. You have to love the Lord who spoke the word and want a genuine relationship with Him. Learning God's word is not a challenge to be met or a task to cross off a to-do list. It is a lifelong commitment to growing in the Lord.
3. Know you will never fully master the word of God. Take the pressure and time limitations off yourself when approaching memorizing scripture. The more you read the word, the more you will get out of it. As we've already studied, the word of God is alive and active. As we grow, we will understand more of it. Memorizing isn't for mastery; it's to help us to navigate through life fully armed to fight the devil.
4. You have to love the word and be willing and able to meditate on the word. To truly study the word, you have to meditate on it. To meditate is to spend time in quiet thought reflecting on the word. It's turning it over in your head. It's breaking down the meaning and weight of each word of a scripture. It means reading the same verse over and over again until you understand it. This not only aids in memory, but in understanding.

There's plenty more to be said about the study of God's word and memorizing scripture. We could talk about the merits and drawbacks of different translations. We could evaluate the accuracy and helpfulness of different commentaries or tools for lexical, topical, and character studies. We could highlight the importance of context and the value of cross referencing. I believe all of these topics are important, but at this stage, the most important thing to share is the importance of diligently studying God's word.

Let's get beyond knowing the general gist of what the word says. Let's get beyond taking another's word about what thus saith the Lord without searching the scriptures for ourselves. Let's get beyond boiling down scripture to cute sayings that don't contain the full power of the word God spoke.

The word is not an accessory. Christ said the words He spoke were Spirit and life. Christ was the word made flesh. He called Himself the life. He came so we may have life and life more abundantly. He wasn't just talking about having material things or experiences like traveling or feeling good; He wanted us to have even more of God's word so we could be brought closer to the source of life and understand following scripture is creating a life—not a lifestyle or worldview, but our entire lives. It gives light to our feet so we can see where we are and a light to our path so we can see the way to where God wants us to go. It is a light darkness flees from.

If we've truly given our lives to Christ, the life He has given us is one more than informed by scripture; it is an embodiment of the scripture. Why do you think marriage is an illustration of the church? To show us and those around us what God wants the church's relationship with Christ to look like! It's the word made visible.

People love to say our lives may be the only Bible people ever read. Have we really stopped to think about the import of this statement? We are supposed to be like Christ, the word made flesh. This bears out the statement. But do we live it?

Are people who look at your life really reading the Bible, or are they reading the latest issue of O magazine? Are they watching Super Soul Sunday? Are they being indoctrinated with positive affirmations written by people who believe the universe is sending them what they need, or karma is avenging them or constraining them? Are people who are reading you reading the truth about God or a lie?

I know some of those questions cut deep. We can become so accustomed to our freedom in Christ we forget everything we are at liberty to do is not expedient, efficient, effective, or impactful in the way it should be. Sometimes our freedom becomes a hindrance or stumbling block to someone else who doesn't understand or doesn't have our level of maturity. We are to think of others before ourselves in this regard. We can't just reflect God's word; we have to live it. It has to live in us.

Sometimes the word will cut us going in and coming out. Sometimes it may cut others no matter how we season our speech with love and speak the truth in love. But just as a surgeon wields his surgical knife to cut out things hurting us, we have to learn to use God's word to cut the sin out to save the whole.

Growth calls for more than one or two meals a week, Sister. I don't give a lot of "rules" or checklist items to ensure growth in this book. But the one thing I must insist you do daily if you want to be serious about growing in God is to eat the word of God daily.

CHAPTER THREE

The Ministry of Me

What obstacles have presented themselves as you've been on this walk with the Lord?

Sis. Zelda Jones: I think the obstacle for me...has been me. The obstacle for me has been me.

The first time anyone told me I had a ministry was at a ladies' day in Brunswick, Georgia. A sister from another congregation had encouraged me to buy a vendor table there to sell my book. I was able to stand before hundreds of ladies and share the heart behind Altered before the Altar: encouraging single Christian women like me to prepare themselves for marriage God's way. Several women came up to my table and said they liked what I was doing and would be praying for my ministry.

My ministry? I looked down at my table in confusion. Did I have a ministry? All I'd done was write a book I knew I needed to read, a book I hoped other women could be challenged and encouraged by. I wasn't a preacher or church leader. I wasn't even a ladies' day speaker. I was just a young woman trying to do what I felt led to do.

Ministry is a word people in the Christian community use frequently but define sparingly. What is ministry? Do you have a ministry? Can you have a ministry? What's involved in doing ministry work?

The word translated as ministry in the New Testament is "diakonía". While diakonía is used in scripture to denote the offices of those who minister, or the people who preach the gospel and/or care for the church, its basic meaning is serviceable labor. Any business or calling whose labor benefits others or displays compassionate love to others is a ministry. You don't have to be a preacher, deacon, elder, or teacher to minister or have a ministry. You don't have to be a male. You can get involved in the various ministries at your church, such as benevolence, door knocking, singles, education, youth, college, senior citizen, widows and orphans, new convert or a variety of others.

When most women think about ministry, they think about serving others. They think about what they can do to help someone else. Indeed, the purpose of ministry is to serve the needs of others. But what many women fail to realize is how intertwined self-care and ministry is.

I believe if we don't understand how God ministers to us, if we don't allow Him to fill us to the point of overflowing, we won't be able to effectively minister to others. Our first ministry work, then, is to understand who God created us to be and what He created us to do. We must know what gifts and talents we have and how they can be used in service to the kingdom. And we have to love and accept ourselves. We have to know God made us a specific way to carry out a specific purpose addressing a specific need in the body of Christ. Our perception of who we are and how God responds to who we are will dictate how we treat others.

The ministry of the Bible and what it has called us to do is both an inward and outward facing ministry. It calls us to work out our soul salvation with fear and trembling (Phil. 2:12) and to be holy as God is holy (1 Pet. 1:15-16). It also calls on us to get outside of ourselves and serve other people. If we're going to be serious about our relationship with God, we must get serious about ourselves and others.

There's no way to be serious about who you are in Christ and what you were called to do/be without loving yourself and saying the things about yourself God says about you in His word. Our attitude about ourselves and who we are needs to be in line with God before we can effectively minister to others. We have to know who and what we are and the One we represent if we are going to make disciples of others.

Many of us struggle to balance these two objectives because we don't realize how one flows into the other. I want to spend some time in this section helping us to reconcile what we are called to do and be for ourselves and others in a way that both makes sense and frees us from both selfishness and impossible standards of service to others.

Ministry starts with us. If we are going to be effective workers in God's kingdom, we have to understand what we are asking people to believe in and follow. This begins with knowing what we are.

So what are we?

1. **We are God's workmanship (Eph. 2:10).** We are created by Him. We are His workmanship created to display and proclaim His glory. You are handcrafted by the hands of God, a one of a kind creation created to serve a universal purpose: to show the Lord's glory to the world.
2. **We are made in His image (Gen 2:15).** We share many of the characteristics of God because He placed them inside of us. God created the world by His word (John 1:1-3); we have the power of death and life in our tongue (Prov.18:21). Yet man comes short of the glory of God (Rom. 3:23). In other words, we are not what God intended for us to be. We have to work to be more like God each day. But we were made to reflect His image. We should look like our Father.
3. **We are fearfully and wonderfully made (Ps. 139:14).** We quote this scripture a lot, but do we know what it means? What does it mean to be fearfully and wonderfully made? The word translated as fearfully in the King James Version is "a very positive feeling of awe or reverence for God which may be expressed in piety or formal worship." Wonderful means miraculous, astonishing, extraordinary. It means "to cause a wonderful thing to happen. This word is used with God as the subject primarily. God does things beyond the

bounds of human powers or expectations. God made us creatures beyond our own expectations." We are something wonderful. We should be in awe of God and worship Him for the incredible gift of life we have. Being fearfully and wonderfully made means you were no accident or after thought. It means you are not an inferior model. Think about it: God, in His power and with His will in mind, set out with intention to make something wonderful, something in His own image designed to illicit worship, praise and a life of piety. At no other point in creation did God make anything else in His own image. We are wonderfully made because our God is wonderful. You were created to be capable of more than you could ever imagine or ask for. No matter how high your expectations of your existence on Earth, God stands ready to do far more.

4. **We are beings God has known since before we were knit together in the womb (Jer. 1.5).** We are people God has a plan for. We are important to God. I'll say this a million times in a million different ways if I have to. *You are not an accident or a mistake.* You aren't mislabeled. Your soul wasn't put with the wrong body. God formed you with His hand. God didn't get the formula wrong when He created you. There is nothing wrong in your creation. Sin corrupts, destroys, warps and impairs. Don't let the world lie to you and tell you God messed you up, or you can't live for Him because being contrary to His will is "just the way you are" or you "were born that way."

5. **We are chosen instruments of God, as God says about Paul (Acts 9:15).** This term can be used to help us understand our role in the Lord better. Paul was commissioned to preach the word to the Gentiles just as we are called to go into all the word, teach, baptize and teach again to the saving of souls (Matt 28:19-20). It's important for us to realize what an instrument is and is not in order to have the proper view of ourselves. An instrument is built for a specific purpose. Instruments can do nothing apart from a musician. They don't

determine what music they are used to play. Instruments respond to the musician's movements. They do what the musician wants them to do when the musician wants them to do it. Instruments aren't praised; it is the musician who gets the accolades and recognition. The musician cares for the instrument, maintaining it, repairing it, and tuning it so it makes the most beautiful music it can. He expects from it only what it was created to do. He doesn't expect a guitar to be able to do what a piano does or for a drum to sound like a flute. He won't play them as if they can. Whether the instrument is a human voice or a manmade instrument, the musician takes care of the instrument and keeps it from getting damaged as much as possible.

6. **We are earthen vessels full of hidden treasure (2 Cor. 4:7).** We are earthen vessels God has made to house His glory and to show Himself. Everything in creation is supposed to reflect God's glory, especially man who is made in His image. No matter what we look like on the outside, we are a plain container whose real treasure is on the inside. God has given us the treasures of the Holy Spirit and His word. The power of His Word is extremely valuable. An earthen vessel doesn't get to determine what it's used for any more than an instrument. Its value comes from what it contains, not what it is made from. It needs to be able to hold the treasure placed within it. A valuable treasure wouldn't be put in a broken vessel where the contents could leak or spill out. No matter how broken you feel, if God has given you His Spirit, His Word, and the blood of Christ has cleansed you from all unrighteousness, you are able to do what God has committed to you to do if you stick with Him. God works in us both to will and do (Phil. 2:13). This means He works in us to create the desire and He works in us to bring about the fulfillment of the desire. We must believe He is faithful to complete the work He began in us (Phil 1:6). We must believe God didn't build us cheaply. We aren't going to break from every little movement or fall. We don't have to cave in

to sin.
7. **We are important to God.** God loved us so much He sent His Son to die for us (Rom 5:8; John 3:16). God is longsuffering because He doesn't want any of us to be lost or to perish (II Pet. 3:9). God's love for us and Christ's love is what should compel us and drive the relationships in our lives (II Cor. 5:14). Everything is compared to God's love for us.

He teaches us about His love for us by telling us that He is our Father. He uses the illustration of the father from the natural world to help us understand facets of His character. We know what a father is supposed to be and what they are supposed to do for their children. God calls us His children and is giving us an inheritance. His love for us as His children is the driving force behind everything God does toward us and what we do in His name, who we are in Him. We are all loved by God.

A Woman's Worth

Everything listed above describing us—the instrument, the vessel, a being God created in His own image—derives a large quantity of its value not from what it is but from who created it. A Stradivarius violin is valuable because Antonio Stradivari created it. A set of pots and pans with Rachel Ray's or Emeril Lagasse's name on it will cost you more than a generic brand because of the name on it. When it comes to assigning value, who made something matters.

We were created by the Creator of all things. We were created by a Creator who makes no mistakes. His name is recognized by everyone. Every knee will bow and every tongue will confess that He is Lord (Phil. 2:9-11, Rom. 14:11). That's who created us. Not the human, fallible people who facilitated our arrival into this world. We are not the product of imperfect people but the creation of a perfect God.

Another way an item's value is determined is by how

much someone is willing to pay for it. As a Christian, you have been bought with a price (I Cor. 6:20, 7:23). That price was the blood of Jesus. The bible says Jesus purchased the church with His blood (Acts 20:28). Jesus believed we were worth dying for. He paid the ultimate price for us. Because Jesus is the one who purchased us, He set our value. We don't get to devalue ourselves or put ourselves on sale. We don't determine our value. The person who did determine our value has given us a price above rubies and gold.

It's hard to go beyond the self when you don't have a proper love and respect for what God has done for you. It's difficult to have low self-esteem when you realize the God of Heaven made you in His image for His purpose beyond the bounds of your powers and expectations. Moreover, He didn't create you and forget about you; He is concerned about you.

Who we are created to be says something about God. Moreover, the things we demonstrate we believe about ourselves show how we feel about the One who created us. As someone who has struggled with low self-esteem, I know how easy it is to get wrapped up in negative thinking about yourself, to beat up on yourself. It wasn't until I realized what my attitude toward myself was saying about what I thought of God that I began to see myself differently.

What are you portraying to the world about God by what you project about yourself? When we complain about being too short or too tall, or our nose being too big or our eyes being too small, we are saying God made a mistake with our appearance. You may think that's too broad a statement, but think about it: when a product has inherent flaws, it is referred to as a manufacturer's defect. Who is your manufacturer? God. So if there is a flaw in your makeup, God made a mistake, right?

People today are quick to say God makes mistakes by how they see themselves and how they live their lives. They believe they were born in the wrong body. They believe they are the wrong sex. They go to doctors to correct God's mistakes with plastic surgery or gender reassignment surgery. We shake our heads and condemn these people to Hell even while we accuse God of making mistakes with how we look or what our bodies can do. We aren't satisfied with the skills and talents we have and we let everyone know it. But at least we haven't started living life as the opposite sex, right?

When we don't value who God created us to be and what He created us to do, we see God through the funhouse mirror of our mind. Who He is becomes distorted by our unmet expectations. Now God is a promise breaker because I don't have the abundant life and peace that passes all understanding He promised me. He's always late because I still don't have the husband, the promotion, or the child I should have had years ago. He shortchanges us because I didn't get all the financial blessings I was supposed to receive or didn't get all the time I should have gotten with my loved one before they died. He doesn't know how to communicate with us because I keep praying and it's like He's not even listening to me. He's a male chauvinist and doesn't like women to be in charge of anything because I'm supposed to be submissive and learn in quietness and not have authority over a man. He's holding me back from being the person I should be for no good reason.

Do you really want to say these things about God? Many of us are saying them to our friends, family, co-workers and sisters and brothers in Christ with our complaints and murmurings. We may not state it so bluntly or want to acknowledge the import of our words, but this is what many of us are living out.

The Greatest Command

How can we expect to grow if we don't know what we will grow to be? The reason I wanted to underline the fact we are made in the image of God is so we can recognize how important it is to know God. We can't know who we are if we don't know who God is.

God made us in His image. He wants us to look like Him and be like Him. If we are His chosen instruments and earthen vessels containing His treasure, then He will use us for His purpose. Shouldn't we know what His treasure is? Shouldn't we know how to let God use us? Shouldn't we know what we are capable of doing in the hands of God? And shouldn't we love and appreciate all He created us to be?

Many Christians have trouble submitting to God because we are scared God will do to us what we have repeatedly done to ourselves. When we don't understand God's nature and how He differs from us, when we bring Him down to a human level, we miss the beauty and safety of submission to His will. Scriptures meant to comfort or bring understanding suddenly become scriptures of stricture and judgment when we don't have things in the proper perspective.

God's word is distorted when viewed and interpreted with no understanding of who God is. His promises can appear false. His love can appear conditional. His words can seem like condemnation and death sentences. His punishments seem too harsh. He doesn't seem understanding of our human frailties and faults. He seems to punish us for being the way He created us. His words appear to be death more than life.

I'm not surprised this happens. When we think of the death we speak in our lives and in our relationships, the limitations and strongholds we perpetuate and buy into with our thinking, it is no wonder we limit God in the same ways. Not knowing who God is and who God created us to be means we can't be partakers in His promises or stewards of the blessings He gives.

Here's the good news: When we understand who God is and read His word correctly, there are a few things we know about ourselves. We know we have value and worth because God says we have value and worth. We were bought with a price! We know the blood of Christ has cleansed us from all unrighteousness and made us meet to be partakers of God's grace. It allows us to be in His presence and be a part of His family. By being obedient to God's word, we have been birthed into the family of God.

But let's not get puffed up. There's a reason the bible commands us to humble ourselves in the sight of the Lord (Jas. 4:10). Our life on Earth is short. It is but a vapor, here one moment and gone the next (Jas. 4:14). This knowledge should humble you. Our bodies, at their strongest, are weak and frail.

There are a lot of things we can't do under our own power. It's only through the sacrifice Christ made on the cross and the Holy Spirit dwelling in our hearts we are able to have a chance at eternal life. We have to depend upon the covering of the blood of Christ to be acceptable in God's sight. It's nothing we have done or could do for ourselves.

Our righteousness is as filthy rags before the Lord. We can't be good enough to earn salvation. We aren't anything that any man should boast. If we are to boast, we should boast in the Lord. God's grace, His unmerited favor, makes us meet to be partakers of the inheritance of the saints in light. An acceptable sacrifice was made to purify us and sanctify us to be able to take on Christ's righteousness.

Having God's word to dwell in us and be written on our hearts enables us to do far more than we could in our own power. Through our power, we will not be able to beat our flesh. There are good things we want to do we don't do and bad things we don't want to do we will keep doing if we are hoping to defeat our fleshly desires on our own. We're going to keep being defeated and beating ourselves up about it.

But take heart! God's strength is made perfect in our weakness. God can be strong in us. He can make us to be strong and courageous if we give our fears and shortcomings to Him. Through Christ not only can we do all things, but we are more than conquerors. We have the ability to tap into so much power in Christ and to be so much greater in Christ, but we have to recognize the source of this power and humble ourselves.

When you have who you are in the proper perspective, you can look to scripture to learn how to love yourself, and therefore others, well. The scriptures give indications of what our love is supposed to look like and how we are to operate in it. Many of these models are based on love of self.

If we don't know how to love ourselves, we'll never love others properly. Many of the commands to love are predicated on how we love ourselves: Love your neighbor as yourself. Love your wives as yourselves. How are we to love our neighbors as ourselves if we don't know how to love ourselves? We will end up treating them with the same disrespect and disregard with which we see ourselves.

The same is true when we look at the commandment Jesus gave His disciples. He told them to love one another as He had loved them (John 13:34-35). If we have a warped view of how Jesus loved us, we can't love others properly. Understanding how God loves us and what His love causes Him to do for us is our roadmap for how to treat one another. If we don't know how God loves us, we are directionless.

Our love for ourselves is an illustration or example of how to love others. Several times in scripture we are told to treat people the way we would like to be treated. We are forgiven by the same measure we forgive others. When we attempt to restore someone we are to remember ourselves and how we were once ensnared in sin. None of this works if our view of ourselves or treatment of ourselves is skewed.

Not knowing how to treat ourselves and love ourselves well may be the reason so many of us can't love others the way we should. If we hold ourselves to impossible standards and leave no room for grace, we will do the same to others. The converse is also true: if we don't hold ourselves to any standard and never tell ourselves the truth in love, we won't call others to repentance either.

The bible says God is not a respecter of persons (Rom. 2:11, Acts 10:34). When it comes to wisdom, James says to ask of God, who gives to all men freely and upbraideth not (Jas. 1:5). Paul says we are no longer Jew, Gentile, slave, free, man or woman but all equal in Christ (Gal. 3:28). The bible speaks of us being one and united with Christ often. Christ prays His followers would be one (John 17:11). In order to love, we must understand we are all loved by God equally. We are equally important and have equal access to

Him if we are in His family.

Unity is essential to carrying out the will of God. In order to be the body of Christ, the individual members have to love each other and work together. They have to recognize and be able to utilize their different skills and talents to the profit of the whole. We must appreciate what everyone brings to the spiritual table and allow those called to specific positions to operate in them.

In our society, we are taught to war against ourselves. We are taught to pick ourselves apart, to look for flaws and deficiencies in our bodies. It is no wonder we do the same thing in the body of Christ! We look for members we think of as weak not to support and help them, but to belittle, ridicule or shame them. We hide certain parts of the body or seek to minimize them. We cover up the damaged instead of healing them. Some we get rid of all together. But we do all of this without the input or directive of our head, Christ Jesus.

How should we treat others in light of this?

The same value we have to God, others have to Him as well. The same way God pursued us and grabbed hold of us, He pursues everyone. The forgiveness and love He's shown us He wants to show others. He wants to use us in His plans to save others. They are just as precious and important to Him as we are.

Just as we don't determine our own value, we don't determine the value of others. The same price that was paid for us was paid for them. We didn't pay that price. We don't own anyone and no one is beholden to us for anything. We need to free others from our expectations and the weight of our disappointment and disapproval. God has freed us from the bonds of sin, and we don't have to be a slave to anyone or anything. God didn't free us for us to go and enslave someone else.

Bottom line: We don't belong to one another. We belong to God. We are to view people the same way we view our bodies: as the property of God. We are merely stewards of this property, doing what the owner has commanded of us to do with it. We are caretakers. We are to take care of one another and build one another up in the Lord until He comes to claim what's His.

CHAPTER FOUR

Ending the Empty Cup Ministry

Too many women are a part of the empty cup ministry. They give so much without putting anything into themselves. Eventually their cup is empty. They continue going through the motions of pouring into those around them, but they aren't adding anything to anyone because they don't have anything to give.

These are the women who grow weary in well doing. They experience burnout. They begin to resent those who always seem to need help. Ministry becomes another obligation they are shackled to instead of a joyful outpouring of the overflow of the love and peace with which God has filled them.

We can't minister to others from the empty cup of our lives.

So how do we go about filling our cup? How do we minister to ourselves? The short answer is, we can't. The very definition of ministry is labor that benefits others or shows compassionate love to others. We've already concluded we are earthen vessels God stores His treasure in. If you are empty, sister, you have to go to God to be filled.

Before you think I tricked you into thinking I had something practical to say to weary women who have poured everything into ministering to those around them, I do have some practical advice. We can't just minister to others; we have to be ministered to ourselves. It's important for us to find those places where we can be shown

compassionate love and be benefited. Here are a few of the places/activities I use to refill my well:
1. **Worship service, revivals, ladies' days, gospel meetings, retreats, or conferences:** Community is key in building us up and equipping us to minister to others. Sit under a minister who rightly divides the Word of God and you'll be amazed how he reads you the book, chapter and verse of your life and shares something that speaks directly to your heart. Attend a ladies' day and see how inspired being around women who are on fire for God makes you. It never fails: when I'm at my driest and emptiest, someone at a worship service or fellowship event says exactly what I need to hear. We can't say we believe God uses us to minister to others and act as if He doesn't use others to minister to us.
2. **Bible study:** I can't tell you how often a verse of biblical example/illustration has come to mind to encourage me in a dry season. The word of God is water to our thirsty souls. A man who meditates on God's law is likened to a tree planted by the rivers of water (Psalm 1:3). Learning to believe in God and abide in Him gives us access to a sweet fulfillment. But if I don't meditate on God's word or become obedient to it, I won't experience rest or refreshment. I won't know what God has to say about rest or what I should be resting from. I can't remember what I don't know. I have to have the word in me in order for it to come out of me.
3. **Prayer:** Prayer is one of the few instances where pouring out fills us up. When we pour out doubt, fear, and anxiety, God can pour in faith, hope and love. We have to empty ourselves of the junk to make room for the abundant life God wants to give us. Sometimes feeling empty means you're full of the wrong stuff. Let's clear it out.
4. **Self-care:** When we take care of our bodies, we feel reenergized and refueled. It's hard to keep

pushing when your physical and mental tanks are empty. Sleep, physical exercise, and eating healthy foods help increase our energy and focus our minds. It's not self-indulgent or a waste of time to look after your health; it's maintaining the temple of the Lord and being a good steward of the body He allows you to h a v e .

5. **What gets you out of bed:** I wake up early to make time for writing and reading. I will sit and talk to a sister about the bible all night. I will binge watch TV shows and movies. I love going to the zoo. I love feeding friends good food while we debate everything from the inane to the life altering. Walking on the trail with my headphones on, holding a happy baby, wandering through a museum, road tripping, taking a million pictures with my camera, eating pasta until I burst—these are some of my favorite things. When I do these things, I feel more able to deal with the daily grind and I'm ready to rejoin my co-laborers in the faith. Whatever makes a late night or an early morning worth it for you, find time to do it. Kiss your husband. Snuggle your baby. Camp in the woods. Eat a s'more. Pet a cat. Read dense discourse on deconstructionism in literature. Make papier-mâché masks. Color in a coloring book. Do what makes your head quiet and your heart light.

CHAPTER FIVE

On the Run

Submit yourselves therefore to God. Resist the devil, and he will flee from you. Draw nigh to God, and He will draw nigh to you. Cleanse your hands, ye sinners; and purify your hearts, ye double-minded. Jas 4:7- 8.

Where are you? Where have you been? Where are you going? What are you doing here? All of these questions are asked to someone who is fleeing or hiding in the bible. There's a difference between fleeing sin and fleeing situations or circumstances. When people flee from people, circumstances, or situations they don't want to deal with, God usually sends them back. Whether they are told to return right away or are sent back forty years later, people are sent back to situations they fled.

Let's dig deeper into this. When we examine the responses given to the above questions, an interesting pattern starts to emerge. The overarching theme in these instances is no one answers the question posed. Yet through these questions, their responses, and the instructions they are given, we can more fully see what our response should be to challenging situations if we want to grow.

"Where are you (Gen. 3:9)?"

This is the question God asks Adam and Eve as He's

walking in the garden. Where is Adam? He's hiding. Adam says "I heard you and I hid because I was naked (v. 10)."

Many of us can relate to Adam. We hide from the voice of the Lord. When we hear something that exposes us and the sin we don't want to acknowledge, we try to hide from it. We don't want people, or God, to see what condition we're in.

The word of God says all things are naked before Him (Heb. 4:13). There is no hiding. Christ came to free us from the fear and shame that causes us to hide from God. He says we shall know the truth, and the truth will set us free (John 8:32).

In order for the truth to free us, however, we have to acknowledge it. God already knows where Adam is, but answering the question is an opportunity for Adam to acknowledge where he is and why. Adam chooses not to tell God where he is. Instead of telling God *where* he is hiding, Adam attempts to explain *why* he is hidden.

How many of us do this when we are found out? Instead of confessing our sin, we want to justify it. We will ignore the freedom in front of us in favor of finding an excuse. Rather than admit we are in sin and our feet carried us there, we excuse our behavior. This limits God's response to us. The bible says if we confess our sins, He is faithful and just to forgive our sins and to cleanse us from all unrighteousness (I John 1:9). But if we don't confess our sins, if we don't repent, God is not going to forgive us.

Because we are prone to give excuses, we are more likely to accept them from others. God didn't do that. He asks follow up questions. "Who told you that you were naked? Have you eaten of the fruit I commanded you not to eat?" Again, God already knows the answer. He is omnipresent and omniscient. None of this happened outside of His sight or knowledge. It's an opportunity for Adam to admit what he has done and take responsibility for his actions. God zeros in on the bit of admission in Adam's response and leads Adam back to confession.

Adam still doesn't choose to take responsibility. He doesn't confess. He places the blame for why he's in this situation on Eve when he made the decision to eat of the fruit. He was there when she did it. He knew where she'd gotten the fruit and why she'd eaten the fruit. The bible says unlike Eve, Adam was not deceived (1 Tim. 2:14). He was fully aware of what he was doing.

It's like that with us sometimes. Sometimes we seek to blame others for things we have willingly done with full knowledge of the possible consequences. Sometimes we even have more knowledge than the people encouraging us to commit the sin. Yet we try to shift blame to everyone else.

In the end, though he never accepts the blame for his part in the fall, Adam is punished along with Eve, whom he implicated, and the serpent, whom she placed the blame on. No one escapes the consequences of their sin, then or now. But the beautiful thing about this example is God had mercy on them. The plan for their salvation was already in place. He gave the earliest prophecy of the coming of Christ in His pronouncement the woman's seed would crush the serpent's head and the serpent would bruise His heel (Gen. 3:15).

Lost and Found

I can't leave this episode of fleeing without focusing in on one important aspect of this story: God looks for and pursues Adam and Eve. This principle is one we find over and over again in God's word. This should solidify and forever settle our love for God. Even when our sin causes us to flee from the face of God, God comes after us.

Christ teaches this principle to His disciples:

> For the Son of man is come to save that which was lost...Even so it is not the will of your Father which is in heaven that one of these little ones should perish. Matt. 18:11, 14

In Luke 15, Jesus speaks a parable to the Pharisees and scribes:

> What man of you, having a hundred sheep if he lose one of them, doth not leave the ninety and nine in the wilderness, and go after that which is lost, until he find it? And when he hath found it, he layeth it on his shoulders, rejoicing. And when he cometh home, he calleth together his friends and neighbors, saying unto them, Rejoice with me; for I have found my sheep which was lost. I say unto you, that likewise joy shall be in heaven over one sinner that repenteth, more than over ninety and nine just persons, which need no repentance. Luke 15:4-7

All of us like sheep have gone astray and turned into our own way (Isa. 53:6). We have wandered and no one but Jesus could come after us because He is our shepherd. Just as God called out to Adam and Eve, Jesus calls out to His sheep. Jesus says His sheep know His voice and will follow Him (John 10:27).

When God calls to us, it gives us an opportunity to realize where we are. More importantly, it establishes where God is in relationship to us. If we can hear Him, He is near. If we will only draw closer to Him, He will draw closer to us. It gives us an opportunity to move closer to Him.

Whenever anything of value is lost, we look for it and we rejoice when we find it. Though both Adam and Eve and the sheep have willfully wandered away and gotten lost, God searches for and pursues them. God is unwilling that any should perish (2 Pet. 3:9). There is rejoicing in Heaven when we respond to God with repentance (Luke 15:7). Whether we come back to God or God pursues us, there is celebration and rejoicing.

A favorite verse of mine says God commended His love toward us, in that, while we were yet sinners, Christ died for us (Rom. 5:8). Even though Adam doesn't reveal himself and come to God, God finds Him. Even though God punishes the sin Adam and Eve committed, He gives all of humanity hope. While man was still in sin and unworthy, God extended love and salvation to us.

If you have run away from God, you must do what the

Prodigal son does in Luke 15:17-20. He came to himself and realized where he was. He realized being the person of lowest degree in his father's house would be so much better than his current situation. God is waiting to welcome you back with open arms and Heaven is ready to rejoice over your return. The question is are you ready to be found? Are you ready to acknowledge where you are and respond to God's call?

"Where have you been and where are you going (Gen. 16:8)?"

Hagar is asked these two questions when she is fleeing Sarai. Hagar responds she is fleeing her mistress Sarai because she is being ill-treated. Instead of telling the angel where she is going, Hagar gives him an explanation for running away. Perhaps Hagar doesn't know where she is going. She has fled from an abusive situation. She may not care where she is going as long as she doesn't have to face Sarai again.

Maybe you've been in a similar situation. Maybe you've fled mistreatment with no idea where you were going. You only knew you couldn't stay where you were a moment longer. Many who flee will say they ***know*** God doesn't want them going through this or that. Instead of trying to search out God's will for a situation, they find an excuse to justify leaving an uncomfortable reality. Instead of taking an honest look at where they've been and where they may possibly be heading, all they see is what they've suffered.

Notice how Hagar doesn't tell him the place where she's been; she tells him about her mistreatment. Her view of her past has shrank down to one facet of experience. Don't we do the same thing sometimes? Don't we tend to focus all of our attention on one aspect of a situation? It's usually the thing we don't like or want to change. The undesirables can become so magnified we can't see any reason to look further.

The angel of the Lord tells Hagar to go back and deal with it. That's the blunt way to put it. He tells her to go back to her mistress and submit herself under her mistress' hands (Gen. 16:9). He doesn't promise her Sarai is going to treat her better or say anything about her situation is going to change. Whether the situation will change or not, Hagar has to get back into position and do what she is supposed to do.

Isn't this an indictment of us? God wants us where He places us. He knows how Hagar has been treated. He knows why she left. But Hagar's flight is not justified by God.

Many Christian women are suffering because they let their emotions dictate when they've had enough. They have gone AWOL, taking action without leave. They have left situations God was not done using to prune them so they could bear even more fruit. They didn't count it all joy or look for the growth resulting from trials. They left where they were supposed to be.

Any time they might be called upon to reflect on where they've been, instead of seeing the place or the positioning, they see their punishment and ill treatment. They stubbornly cling to the idea of a new place when God is telling them to go back and submit under their Master's hands. The blessing of God they left to seek? It's not out there; it's in the place they have left.

Even though I said "they," sister, I'm talking about us, about me. At one time or another, we've all been guilty of fleeing instead of submitting.

I didn't mention the reason behind Hagar's ill-treatment. Hagar was mistreated because of how she was treating Sarai. When she knew she was pregnant, Hagar despised Sarai (Gen. 16:4). She looked down on her. She thought she was better than Sarai because she conceived and Sarai could not. Sarai's response wasn't right, but Hagar's mistreatment originated with how she had treated another woman.

How many times could a situation have turned out differently if I had just kept my mouth shut? How many times could something have gone a lot smoother if I hadn't disrespected someone else? How often am I fleeing the consequences of my actions while proclaiming God wouldn't want me to go through this?

Here's the wonderful thing about this story. Genesis 16:7 says the angel of the Lord found Hagar. God sent one of His angels to locate her. Isn't it amazing how God looks for us when we've gotten out of position? Isn't it amazing He seeks to restore us? Isn't His mercy and redemptive love unfathomable? Even when we have done wrong and fled from the consequences of our wrongs, God is not only open to receiving us back, He sends someone to look for us.

Not only does the angel of the Lord find Hagar to send her back, he lets her know God has seen her affliction. God has seen her mistreatment. He promises her seed will be multiplied (v. 10). Hagar is in awe of the fact God sees her. She names the fountain where she encountered the angel Beer-lahai-roi, the well of Him that liveth and seeth me (v. 13-14).

God sees us in our afflictions, even when we've brought them upon ourselves. God is not confused or "out of the loop" about what's going on in our lives. When we think about where we've been and where we are going, no matter what is behind us or before us, we have to know God is right here with us in this moment. God sees us and He hears us.

If we have truly surrendered control of our lives to God and are operating in His will, we need to accept God knows what He's doing. We have to submit ourselves under His hands. Don't leave the place where God is because of how you feel. Let God finish the work He began in you in the place He designated to do the work.

It's not a matter of God not seeing and hearing us but a matter of us not seeing and hearing Him. Don't let your situation appear so big and unconquerable you don't believe God can use what was meant to destroy you to purify you.

"What are you doing here (I Kgs. 19:9)?"

This question is asked of Elijah when he flees Jezebel.

Jezebel has sworn to kill him in retribution for the slaughter of the prophets of Baal. Elijah journeys forty days and nights into the wilderness to Mt. Horeb, where the voice of God comes to him and asks this question. Twice.

It's interesting to me God asks Elijah this twice.

Most of the time when we ask someone what are they doing somewhere, it's because we didn't expect them to be where they are. It wouldn't require an explanation if they were where they were supposed to be.

Have you ever found yourself in a situation and wondered what you were doing in it? Nothing in your life has suggested you would be where you ended up. This is the situation Elijah finds himself in.

Earlier in the text, Elijah sits under a tree and says he wants to die (v. 4). He says this is enough. I've had it. I may as well not even be here if this is how my life is going to go. He has left his servant behind and journeyed into the wilderness to ask God to take his life. This is a man who has reached the end of his rope and is in true despair.

Yet when God asks him what he's doing there, he doesn't tell God he wants to die. Instead of asking for anything, Elijah begins to complain. Elijah tells God what he has done. He tells God what the children of Israel have done. He insists he is the only prophet of God left and they are after his life as well. This is pure complaint.

Elijah has just caused fire to rain down from the heavens and slew the prophets of Baal (I Kgs. 18:36-40). He has stood up mightily for the Lord. He has seen for himself the great power God has placed in his hands as a prophet and ambassador for the Lord. Why, then, does he run at the first word from Jezebel? What makes him so afraid?

We witness this over and over again in scripture. A great victory will be followed by a stunning defeat or low point in the person's/nation's history: the children of Israel brought down the walls of Jericho and took the city, only to be killed and routed back by the tiny town of Ai; after defeating the Ammonites and the Syrians, David sins with Bathsheba; after having a king or two who did what was right in the sight of the Lord, the next king would do what was evil in the sight of the Lord.

There seems to be a special vulnerability people are subject to after they have accomplished something great in God. They forget who gave them the victory. They stop doing what they are supposed to do. They get bored. They forget. Or like Elijah, they flee at the first sign of opposition. Elijah airs all of his grievances, but he doesn't ask the Lord to do anything. God is all powerful. Why doesn't he ask God to defeat his enemies? Why doesn't he ask God to show him what to do? Why doesn't he ask God to raise up more prophets? Because complaining is its own reward.

When we complain to others, oftentimes our complaining is rewarded with sympathy or even praise for our ability to keep the faith. Man will make much of us for "being real" about our struggles. They will puff us up and make us feel as if we have a right to feel the way we do.

But God isn't there for Elijah's whining—literally. God sends a powerful wind, an earthquake and a fire before Elijah, but God isn't in any of it. Then God again asks Elijah why he's there. Elijah is so caught up in his despair he repeats the same line of reasoning to God. He still doesn't ask God to do anything.

God doesn't address Elijah's sentiments. God sends Elijah on to the next mission He wants Elijah to complete. It's only after He gives Elijah these instructions that God informs Elijah he is not alone. God still has many followers in the land.

Sometimes we feel as if we are the only ones living for God. We feel as if we are fighting against the whole world. We will have great victories only to find more battles to fight. We get tired and we get tempted to complain. We may think to ourselves "what's the use of even trying? Every time I try to do the right thing and fight off one temptation or endure one trial, a bigger one comes along." We may feel isolated and alone. Depression may set in. We may lose sight of who God is and what He can do. We will stop asking Him to show up in our lives and help us when we stop believing He cares about us.

But we must be careful with complaining and

overgeneralizations. The bible speaks expressly against complaining (Phil. 2:14; I Cor. 10:10). Complaining is a sin. It makes God angry. We are supposed to give thanks in all things (I Thess. 5:18) and count it all joy (James 1:2), knowing God is working in us through the things worldly people complain about.

Instead of complaining, we must be like Bartimaeus (Mark 10:32-34). When Jesus asks Bartimaeus what he wants Jesus to do for him, Bartimaeus answers immediately, specifically, and with total conviction Christ can do what he is asking. We don't know how long Bartimaeus was blind or how long he sat by the roadside begging, but when Jesus came by, he called out to Jesus. He asked Jesus to have mercy on him. Unlike the lame man by the pool, Bartimaeus didn't meet the Lord with complaints, excuses or an attitude of resignation toward his circumstances, but with a humble request delivered in faith. We can't grow weary and give up, Sisters. We can't run away from the tests and trials inherent in being a child of God. The one thing Elijah does right is going into the wilderness by himself to meet with God. He was empty and discouraged in a way he didn't know how to bear up under, but He knew God could do something about it.

God didn't do what Elijah wanted God to do. He didn't allow Elijah to run away from life. He didn't let Elijah die. He gave Elijah purpose and encouragement. He let Elijah know he was not alone.

We aren't alone, sisters. Every woman who tries to live for God is surrounded by a cloud of witnesses to God's faithfulness to His promises (Heb. 12:1) and is part of a community of called out believers. Despite how we feel, God is with us.

Go Back and Try it Again

God sent Moses back to Egypt forty years after he fled the country. Moses fled because he killed an Egyptian who was beating a Hebrew. After this, Pharaoh tries to kill Moses, so he flees for his life (Ex. 2:11-15). God tells Moses to go back. Moses begins making excuses like everyone else. "I'm not great at speaking (Ex. 4:10)," etc. The thing I find interesting is God listens to all of the grievances Moses has and responds to them. I think we miss this today in many ways.

Can you imagine what it must be like to flee from someone who is mistreating you or someone seeking to kill you, to finally have an audience with God—and God sends you back to the situation you fled? You've run away because you feel threatened and in danger. You didn't leave because you grew bored. And our awesome, amazing Father sends you back. When we aren't sent out by God but are fleeing situations, God sends us back.

Doesn't it suck that when we run away, God sends us back? We still have to go confront the thing we fled. God ministers to us. He lets us get our feelings out. He will reveal more of His plan to us or more of who He is or let us see what's happening beyond our immediate reality. He prepares us more fully for what is to come. But He always sends us back.

So many of us are trying to cut out early, to "move on" when God is telling us to go back. We aren't finished there. He still has more for us to do or learn there.

Fight or Flee?

Let's be clear: there are some things we have to flee. The bible say to flee sin. We are to flee fornication (I Cor. 6:12, 18), idolatry (I Cor. 10:14), youthful lusts (2 Tim. 2:22), and the love of money and desire to be rich (1 Tim. 6:9-10). Christ says His sheep will flee the voice of a stranger (John 10:5). Indeed, there are times we need to flee.

But there are other times when the bible tells us to fight. The bible says to resist the Devil and He will flee from us (Jas. 4:7). We see this in action when the Devil tempted Christ in the wilderness. When Jesus resisted the devil, he retreated for a season (Luke 4:13).

The issue many of us have is we don't know

when to fight and when to flee. Any time we feel uncomfortable, mistreated, stagnant, threatened, bored, or fearful, we think we need to move. I have to do something. I have to go somewhere else. I need to do something new. I can't just sit here and let myself be mistreated.

When anything interrupts the smooth flow of our lives, when anything throws us slightly off course, we are ready to start doing. Maybe this book was bought out of your need to do something, to change things up, to get out of a place you feel stuck in spiritually. But the biblical example seems to be if it isn't sin you're stuck in, no matter how many times you flee, it will find you. Not only will it find you, God will send you back to deal with it His way.

God's way is to confront difficult situations. God's way is for us to press in to those feelings and figure out what we're supposed to get out of our circumstances. Like Jacob, we have to wrestle with our hardships and not let go until we are blessed from the situation and can see God's hand at work in it (Gen. 32:24-28). We have to wait.

When we wait with expectation and a surrendered will, professing we know God is with us; when we ask God to show up in the middle of the mess and make the way out clear as only He can, we invite Him in. Oftentimes in tough situations, Jesus is standing at the door of our heart knocking, and if we will let Him in, He will come and sup with us (Rev. 3:20). We will have sustenance that gives us strength and communion with Him that gives us peace, but we have to invite Him in.

God is clear in His word when He asks people to follow His leading into situations where they may feel fear, discomfort, or inadequacy. He always lets the person He is leading into these dark places know He is with them.

Let's stand in this knowledge for a moment. God, who always was and always will be; who is all knowing, all powerful and everywhere all at once; who the winds and waters obey; who is over all and in all; who can use those who don't even acknowledge His existence to accomplish His will; who ordered all history; who has defeated every foe—this God says He will be with me in the hard places where I'm pressed on every side and fear grips me and pulls me in close to its side. He will be with me when I'm so close to death I'm walking in its shadow (Psalm 23:4). He will never leave me or forsake me. What was I worried about again?

Paul asks "who can separate us from the love of God? (Rom. 8:35)" He lists hardships like tribulation, famine, distress, and persecution. But he insist we can be more than conquerors in all these things (Rom. 8:37). Nothing can separate us from the love of God but sin we refuse to repent of. We can conquer any circumstance or situation through Christ. We don't have to flee.

Sin must be cut off. God didn't send anyone back into sin. What we are discussing are instances of people fleeing *situations*, not sins. People became uncomfortable or fearful and fled.

When Pharaoh scoffs at Moses and makes the people's work harder, the people reject Moses. They don't want Moses speaking or doing things on their behalf. God still sends Moses back. He still has more to accomplish to the glory of God. If we are letting God direct us, sometimes we have to go back to some situations or stay in some situations we don't want to be in.

This is different from how we should deal with sin. We are to flee sin. The bible says all over the place to flee sin and temptation. We shouldn't try to stand stalwart against it or fight back against it. But when we are confronted with an unpleasant situation, many times we are asked to stay and endure.

These situations grow us. Sometimes these situations are for people beyond us, but they are *always* for us. **They grow us.** They teach us to trust God to move us where He wants us. They teach us to allow Him to do things in our lives instead of trying to accomplish them ourselves. They teach us to do what He tells us to do, which can be difficult because our instincts are telling us to do something completely different. Fear takes hold of us. Doubt gets a hold on us. Our fight or flight response kicks in and we want to flee. It's a human reaction.

God understands our human tendencies. He understands we have feelings about the situations we find ourselves in. The fact God hears the concerns and listens to the feelings of these examples of fleeing people shows His care and concern. But He still wants us to do what He sent us to do.

We're not able to flee long term. God always sends you back if you're not ready, or haven't learned what you needed to learn from the situation. Jacob needed to confront Esau after years of running away from him. Jacob had to confront Laban after he left with his wives and all their belongings. We can run all we like, but at some point, we have to own up to what we've done or stand up for what we believe.

We may avoid doing something for a while, but if we want to continue to grow, we'll have to do it eventually. The children of Israel avoided entering the Promised Land for forty years. They still had to go the same way into the same land to fight the same nation they would have fought the first time God told them to do it. Now it's forty years later. People have died instead of moving forward. Will you die in the wilderness because you still haven't learned to trust God at His word and move forward in faith when He tells you to?

God sees us where we are, even when we hide or flee. Even when we're not where we're supposed to be, God sees us. This is something we need to notice and be encouraged by. No one's in a situation, predicament, or circumstance God doesn't see. Whether we think our circumstances are trivial compared to what other people might be going through, or we feel as if we're going through much worse than what everyone else is going through, God sees our struggle. God hears it. God is concerned about it.

But is God involved? For some of us, He is not involved because we haven't involved Him. We may be in sinful situations or otherwise outside of His will. God sees this, too. If God always sees us in our insignificant, drop in the bucket, nobody will remember in a hundred and fifty years lives, then what we are doing, why we're doing it, where we are, where we've been, and/or where we're going is important to God. It should be even more important to us.

Deep Roots & Producing Fruit

If you can't survive in almost any conditions, if your circumstances have to be almost pristine, has to be perfect, for you to survive, there's a good chance you're not going to survive. If you have to be fertilized by someone else. If you have to be watered by someone else. If you have to be motivated by someone else, it's a good chance you're not going to be motivated. ~Bro. Maurice Blackmon

What's the point of all this? The point is you cannot grow when you're running away from God and His plan for your life. You have to be rooted to grow. Jesus described it best to His disciples when He explained the parable of the sower:

> [20]But he that received the seed into stony places, the same is he that heareth the word, and anon with joy receiveth it; [21]Yet **hath he not root in himself** but dureth for a while: for when tribulation or persecution ariseth because of the word, by and by he is offended. Matt. 13:20-21 (emphasis added)

Roots are vital to growth. They regulate the acquisition and disbursement of nutrients throughout the plant, keep the plant anchored, support the plant and even tell the shoots how fast they can grow. Plants can adapt to seasonal changes, but roots grow to *specific conditions*. Any change in the condition of the roots' environment can impede the plant's growth.

As Christians, we have to be rooted, or planted in our conviction of who God is and what He has done for us. We have to be convinced beyond a shadow of a doubt God is in the midst of all things and working to bring about good for us (Rom 8:28). We must be rooted and grounded in love (Eph. 3:17).

Our roots are what will pull nutrients, the water and

bread of the word, from our hearts to grow us in difficult times. Those roots will keep us anchored so we won't be uprooted or knocked down by every storm we find ourselves weathering. Our roots determine how much we are going to grow.

We must let God's word take root in our heart and keep us from being tossed around by every wind of change, sisters. We can't run when it gets hard and expect to flower or bear fruit.

Our roots need a consistent environment. We can deal with the changing of seasons if our roots remain planted in the same soil, with access to the same nutrients. Don't destroy your opportunity to grow and bear fruit because of what you feel; stay rooted in what you know.

As previously stated, the soil in the parable of the sower is the heart of the person. The environment for our roots, our heart, must be a consistent environment. James 4:16-17 tells us in order to resist the devil, we must be submitted to God. It also says our hearts must be purified. We can't be double-minded. We can't follow God today and give up on Him tomorrow and not expect our wavering to impede our growth.

Planting the seed of the word in the ground of your heart and letting it take root does nothing if your heart isn't a stable environment for the roots. An unsettled heart is an impediment to growth. Give your roots a stable environment. Stop running from the Lord and His pruning, Sister. Trust the vinedresser to purge you so you can bear more fruit.

CHAPTER SIX

Glory to... Who?

> Let your light so shine before men, that they may see your good works, and glorify your Father which is in heaven. Matt. 5:16

> For all have sinned and come short of the glory of God. Rom. 3:23

As Christians, we hear about God's glory all the time. We may even say "Glory to God" or "To God be the glory" when something good happens. But do you really know what it means to glorify God? How do we glorify Him? Can we glorify Him when things don't go well, when we don't get the outcome we expect or the thing we pray for? How do we learn to glorify God in every season of our lives if every season isn't going to be shareworthy on social media?

There is a distinction between giving God glory and giving God praise. Many of us operate as if this is the same thing. In doing so, we sometimes fail to give God glory in situations where we can't find gratitude or thanksgiving as easily. We struggle to see the positives we can thank God for in hard places with little light. But thankfulness and praise are not synonymous with glory.

What does it mean to glorify God? The dictionary definition of glorify is to honor or praise. We understand praise. But what about honor? The term glorify in the New Testament is often translated from the word "Doxa." Doxa means we are giving recognition belonging to a person, honor, renown. It means to bring honor. In reference to God, it means to recognize God for who He is. We glorify God by recognizing who He is and being what He intended for us to be. When we conform to God's image and character, we show the world who He is.

When the bible says people will see our good works and glorify our Father in Heaven, it not only means they will praise God because of what we have done but they will recognize something of the character of God through us. When we give God the proper credit for what He has done through us, people can correctly attribute to God what He is able to do with a surrendered heart and will. When we can have peace in the midst of a trial, we can show God gives peace and there is rest in His presence. When we are obedient to Him and reap the rewards of our obedient faith, others can see God does reward those who diligently seek Him and He does keep His word.

We are God's representatives on Earth. Our lives need to tell others about Him. Even in our disappointments and grief, we should show God is good.

When the Bible says man comes short of the glory of God, it means man is not what God intended him to be. God said "Let us make man in our own image (Gen. 1:26)", but we are not as like God as we were intended to be. Sin was introduced and separated us. We lack much of God's image and character. In response, God sent His Son Jesus, the Word that was with Him from the beginning and by whom all things were created, to the world to live as a man and show us what we were intended to be.

Christ is our example for how to live in this world in anticipation of the next. He showed us how to reflect God's glory. Christ constantly pointed back to His Father in Heaven. Everything He did was to help people recognize who God is, what He does, and what He requires. He came to save us by pointing us back to God and making a relationship with Him possible.

Jesus wasn't always recognized as the Son of God. Though many believed on Him, others sought His life for His claims to be the Son of God. As Christians, our lives are to shout the message Jesus was the Son of God who came into the world He created to die for our sins so we could be adopted as sons and daughters. His sacrifice made it possible for us to be partakers and co-heirs of the inheritance of God. If no one else will recognize Christ for who He was on Earth and is in Heaven, then we must. Our lives must point back to Him.

If the only thing about you giving recognition to the Lord is your mouth, there is a problem. Jesus doesn't say people will hear us say to glorify God and they will glorify Him. He says our good works will lead others to glorify God. We don't have to say anything. They see what we are doing and they know to glorify God for it.

Make no mistake: everyone who claims to be a Christian needs to be ready in season and out of season to give a reason for their faith (II Tim. 4:2) and teach those in the world about Jesus. But our lips shouldn't be the primary source of glory. Jesus says the people draw nigh to me with their lips but their hearts are far from me (Matt. 15:8). James says we ought not to bless God out of the same mouth we curse men which are made after the similitude of God (Jas. 3:9-10).

What we say matters, but it matters in totality. Our mouths don't need to spread confusion about who God is by saying things contrary to His character. If Christ truly dwells in our hearts, His word will come out of our mouths.

There is a strong connection between what's in our hearts and what comes out of our mouths. It's referenced over and over again in scripture. Our heart's true nature is exposed by our tongue. People may say things with their lips and have something else in their hearts. By having a show of godliness they may fool man, but God knows when our hearts are far from Him.

We need to examine ourselves. Is the truth of what you say you believe reflected in how you live your life? If people need your words to identify your faith, it's time to reevaluate your life.

Motivation is also important when we talk about glorifying God. When we do things to be seen, we have our reward. God sees our hearts, whether we perform acts that appear to give God praise or honor, such as fasting, prayer, or giving to the poor, or we do things against His word such as murmuring, complaining, cursing, stealing, cheating, etc. He knows where we stand, whether it is at a distance from Him or walking right beside Him. I'm not saying we can murmur, complain, or steal with right motives. Sin is sin. The comparison is made to show how so-called holy acts, when done to be seen of men instead of to grow a relationship with God and get the strength we need to live out our convictions of who He is, can be just as vain and ineffectual as not doing what God has required of us.

Are you using everything you don't have to glorify God? Are you using the things you want but don't currently have, the things you are working for but aren't yet seeing come to fruition, to glorify God? Are we using those areas of bareness or barrenness to glorify God? Is it possible to do this? If so, how do we accomplish it?

As I've shared earlier in this chapter, to glorify God is to recognize Him for who He is. It's also to recognize how we've fallen short of what we were created to be. All the honor and accolades belong to God. If we are going to show God's glory in areas where we lack or fall short, it is by proclaiming through word and deed the goodness of God and making sure people see God for who He is despite our current situation or circumstance.

I have a hard question for you: do you want *God* to get the glory in your life, or do *you* want to get the glory? Is your life in line with what you just professed? Are you living this or just saying it? All of creation, both heaven and earth, reflect God's glory. We should be no different. Not for God's benefit, but for our own. He will be praised. If we keep our peace, the rocks will cry out (Lk. 19:40).

Yet sometimes we, the only part of creation God made in His image, refuse to reflect God's glory in favor of coveting glory for ourselves. We want people to look at us, to like us, to follow us. Sometimes we may say "follow me as I follow Christ," but we really mean "follow me like you would follow Christ."

Wanting to be seen or recognized for what we do instead of trying to get others to see Jesus and the Father is a major hindrance to truly glorifying God. Jesus speaks expressly against doing things before men, to be seen of men, or to appear a certain way to men (Matt 6:2, 5, 16). God says those people have their reward. You don't need to look for a reward from God when you've sought glory and recognition for yourself among men.

Regarding the spiritual disciplines of prayer, fasting and almsgiving, Jesus exhorts us to do them secretly and allow God to reward us openly (Matt 6:3-4, 6). Only your Father in Heaven needs to know what you are doing because you are doing it for Him and the relationship you wish to cultivate with Him. If you are fasting, you need to wash your face and fix your hair (Matt. 6:17). Keep your mouth shut about it. Don't take pride in telling someone you can't eat this or that because you are fasting to garner their admiration. Don't complain about being hungry or paint yourself as a martyr. Let the thing you are fasting for be between you and God. This way, when He rewards you openly, you can know of a surety it is from Him and not something your machinations brought about.

We don't want to be confused: **spiritual discipline is not suffering in silence.** It's not suffering, period. Cultivating a spiritual discipline is seeking after God and pursuing Him. It should not be associated with suffering. Yes, all those who will live godly must suffer persecution (II Tim. 3:12), but living a godly lifestyle is not the source of the suffering. God give us abundant life, life that overflows and fills others up. Spiritual discipline helps us to access abundant life by building a relationship with God and seeking to understand Him. We suffer because we live in a fallen world ruled by Satan. The relationship we build with God through spiritual discipline gives us the strength to bear suffering and persecution.

Suffering comes in when we pretend as if we don't care about the areas of lack in our lives but we're inwardly struggling with them. Bitterness can breed in us when we want something and we don't receive it within our timeframe.

As believers, we are taught to believe in God. God is the giver of all good and perfect gifts (Jas. 1:17). When we don't get what we want, we can become frustrated with God. We can try to cover it with cute sayings and an appearance of godliness, but the odor of our discontent wafts all around us, telegraphing our falsity to others.

We can't help it. We put on a brave face and try to mask it, but then we cry out not only to God but to anybody who will listen to us about the things we don't have. "God, you said you would give me the desires of my heart, but my heart is desiring this and you won't give it to me. You said if I ask for it then I'll receive it, but I've been asking for this and you haven't given it to me yet." We may say we are waiting on the Lord, but people can see by our actions we aren't being patient.

We may adopt an attitude reflecting the belief God helps those who help themselves and start trying to "help" God. We begin researching ways to bring about what we want to happen, stalking blogs and websites, straining social connections and relationships, bombarding people with our presence, and forcing our agendas on any unsuspecting person who might be able to bring us one step closer to what we want. We get aggressive about going after what we lack instead of running after God. We let what we don't have hijack our focus. It becomes bigger than everything else in our lives.

All of which is seen by other people. While our mouths may say we are content with Jesus alone, they see the way we act and the other things we say aren't lining up with our convictions. We ruin our witness to other people when we do this.

What is a witness? A witness is someone who saw something and is willing to testify about it. A good witness is consistent and certain of what they saw and heard. They don't rely on what someone else saw or heard; this is called hearsay and is not admissible in a court of law. You can only testify about what you have personally experienced.

Lawyers look for witnesses who are confident and not easily confused. They look for people who convey conviction in their statements. They want someone people will believe is telling the truth.

We should exhibit the same characteristics when witnessing to non-believers. We should be telling people what we know, what we have experienced. If you want to bring people to Jesus, you have to be strong in your position and conviction. Your story has to be consistent.

If God is good, let Him be good. Don't make Him an unjust entity who withholds good things from you, or portray Him as a liar who makes promises He doesn't keep by how you respond to lack in your life. You're showing you don't believe God and you're inwardly becoming bitter toward Him.

Sometimes we take the promises of God out of context. The bible does say God will give us the desires of our heart but there's a condition. We get the desires of our heart *if* we delight ourselves in Him (Psalm 37:4). Sometimes our desires don't align with delighting ourselves in the Lord. There are activities we desire which don't align with delighting ourselves in the Lord. Delighting ourselves in the Lord may change our desires. A heart delighting in the Lord will desire His will and His plans.

It's the same thing with promises such as ask and you shall receive. Sometimes we ask and receive not because we ask with selfish motives, to spend on our lusts (Jas. 4:3). If we are only asking for things to benefit ourselves and quench our selfish desires, we may not receive it. If we are asking with doubting instead of faith, if we are wavering, we shouldn't expect God to do anything for us (Jas. 1:6-7).

Yes, God does make even our enemies to be at peace with us, but this happens when our ways please God (Prov. 16:7). *The results come after the requirement is fulfilled.* Our enemies won't be at peace with us until our ways please God. We can't have it the other way around. God is not obligated to give us the promised reward if we aren't doing the agreed upon work. It's like expecting to get a paycheck from someone you've never worked for. We are subject to the terms and conditions of the covenant. God will fulfill His promises when we meet His requirements.

"I'm supposed to have peace that surpasses all understanding, but I don't feel peaceful." Are we doing what gives us the kind of peace that surpasses all understanding? Are we giving God our burdens and leaving them at His feet to take the weight off ourselves? Or are we telling God what's bothering us but still trying to figure it out?

We can't feel less weighed down if we don't put anything down. We lay our burdens down in prayer but pick them back up when we continue to worry about them and try to think of ways to fix things ourselves. Every time we leave God's presence we feel the weight fall back on our shoulders.

Where God gets the glory in barrenness or our not getting what we want when we want it is when other people can see this positive or different spirit about us and they want to know where it came from. When people can see a childless couple who longs for a child being content in their lack, they will wonder what the couple's secret is. How are they not being driven crazy by what they don't yet have? How can they be genuinely happy for others who are receiving the thing they are longing for?

They may ask you how you're able to be as happy or as content as you are with this area of lack. This is an opportunity for you to introduce them to God. You can promote God and allow Him to get glory from the situation.

But if someone asks you how you're able to cope and you say things like "I'm just trying to keep it together" or other self-centered statements suggesting you're doing it by your own power, you lose your opportunity to give God glory. The person won't be able to recognize God for who He is because instead of showing them God, you're showing them your strength. When they congratulate you on your perseverance or say they wish they could be like you, you have your reward. God didn't get any glory from the situation.

God wants to be seen as God. He wants people to see what the Lord has done. God is the one who gets the glory from this. God is the one who should because He's the one doing it.

If we have the desires of our heart when we want them, we may feel as if we made it happen. If we first have to start trusting in God and leaning on Him to supply our needs, we're more likely to give Him the glory. We are more likely to say, "I really want this job, but Lord you're my provider. I recognize you'll provide for me according to your will." We are more likely to tithe from the money we receive from our job when we can reflect on God's provision for us when we were unemployed or underemployed. We can genuinely give God the glory He deserves when people recognize what we have.

But do we really want to do that? So many of us battle with wanting to be recognized for what *we* have done and refuse in word or deed to share the glory with God, let alone give *all* the glory to Him.

Wanting to be acknowledged and valued by others is a fundamental fight with the flesh. We have to stay close to God and in His word to keep reminding ourselves of the great value we have in Christ. We have to seek our worth where genuine worth may be found.

We have a price. Jesus paid it. He purchased us with His blood. There can be no higher value placed on you than that. We don't need to look any further for validation.

God bought us with a price; don't make yourself a slave to men and their opinions (I Cor. 7:23). Don't enslave yourself to the perception you have to do it all. When we let God be God, He can do the impossible. And when people see what He's done for us, we can give Him the glory He deserves.

CHANGING SEASONS

Bare Branches & Barren Believers

There's no such thing as a faithful Christian who is stagnant or isn't growing. –Harvey Drummer Jr., Minister

We see this principle at work in the Bible: if we abide in Christ as Christ abides in the Lord, we will produce fruit and have life no matter the situation because of who God is—not because of our circumstances, who we are, what we have done, or what we have suffered. Bearing fruit, being productive, and changing for the better is for the glory of God. Receiving good and perfect gifts from the Lord is for God's glory.

But what about those areas in which we aren't producing fruit or haven't seen growth? Does lack of fruit in an area mean we aren't abiding in Christ? Is there a difference between being bare, without fruit for a season, and being barren, unable to produce fruit? How are we to function when we are bare or barren, when others can't see any fruit in our lives in a certain area? What are we supposed to do with areas where we lack growth?

One of the principles of barrenness, or a key takeaway when God allows areas of barrenness in our lives, is there are cravings we have which can only be fulfilled or satisfied by God. When we experience lack and allow the experience to propel us to seek Him, God shows us He provides us with everything, not just what we believe we can't do for ourselves, But sometimes our lack is not only for us to realize we need Him. Sometimes having insufficiencies and weaknesses are to show God's strength, grace, and glory to those around us still lost in sin.

The bible says let everything that has breath praise the Lord (Ps. 150:6). When you are sick, grieving, or suffering spiritual, emotional, mental or financial barrenness or lack, you still have breath. You still need to be recognizing God for who He is. If I am sick, I can glorify God by recognizing Him as The Great Physician. I can reflect a strong belief that God's will is being done in my life and seek to learn what God would have me to learn from this season of sickness. Whether He decides to cure me or not, I can know this is going to bring about good.

When I lose a loved one, I can recognize God is close to the brokenhearted (Psalm 34:18) and that Jesus wept like we do when His friend Lazarus died. Weeping and sadness doesn't mean we don't believe God is God or His perfect will has been done; it means we are sad. Even in our sadness, we can show our belief God is good and He binds up our wounds. He consoles us. Whenever we draw close to Him, He draws close to us (Jas. 4:8). No matter who is removed from our lives in whatever manner, God never leaves nor forsakes us and He is faithful to finish the work He began in us.

The condition of barrenness exposes our character. How we respond to being unfruitful in an area of our lives shows us something about who we really are. It is easy to proclaim to love the Lord when we perceive He is giving us good things, but what do we become when we feel empty, depleted, forgotten, or punished? Do we draw close to God when we recognize lack in our lives and seek His will, or do we become bitter? Are we taking our requests to God or trying to get what we want in our own power?

Most of us have experienced barrenness at one time or another. If you don't seek to understand the point of being bare or barren in a particular area of your life for a particular season, you will struggle to grow in this season. If your sole or primary focus is on getting back to normal or presenting a certain picture to the world, you won't be able to understand why God wanted you to be bare for a season. If you don't care why you aren't producing fruit but are more concerned with how it looks to others that you aren't producing fruit, you will miss the benefit of God purging you in the first place. God purges or cleanses us so we can bear more fruit, not to keep us unfruitful. Don't miss out on growing by chasing the outward appearance of growth.

The reason for bareness or barrenness is not always tied to our motivation. We can also be bare or barren because God is doing something with us in the season we're in for His glory. We are not being *punished* by God but *perfected*. In agriculture, there are periods where the earth must lay fallow in an area for the earth to regain its nutrients and be rich, fertile soil able to support the growth of a crop. If the soil of your heart is depleted, if it's not enriching ground to plant in, you have to be fallow for a while. God may remove certain people or commitments from your life which are stripping your heart of love, draining your resources, or stealing your focus.

God never gives us things we are not prepared for. He doesn't even allow us to be tempted above what we can bear. Sometimes He calls us to pull away from striving and output to rest for a while and be reenergized by Him. Sometimes we need to pull away and cultivate our hearts in preparation for what God wants to plant and bring forth next.

Sometimes farmers will rotate crops to resupply nutrients to depleted soil. If a crop has stripped the soil of a particular nutrient, they will plant a crop in the stripped soil chosen to replace the missing nutrients. The new crop uses different components of the soil to grow. Maybe God has planted a crop of rewarding friendships in your life to replace the love in your heart depleted by too many bad romantic relationships. Maybe God is allowing you to develop more appreciation for the time and money you have by placing more opportunities in your life to visit the elderly or volunteer with homeless shelters instead of providing you with opportunities to spend those resources on trips.

Perhaps our focus has been too much on bearing fruit and harvesting without focusing on what kind of fruit we are bearing or what type of harvest we will be reaping. Maybe we've been producing great crops but we are stripping the soil of vital nutrients with overwork. You don't want to grow weary in well doing (Gal 6:9). God calls us to rest in Him, to worship Him, to recognize and glorify Him.

We can't forget the point of everything we do is to bring glory and honor to God and to live out His will in our lives, not to reach a certain status or effect a certain amount of change.

There is nothing wrong with having godly goals or wanting to be fruitful. There's nothing wrong with wanting to spread the gospel message and bring others to the knowledge of Christ and salvation. Those are things we are commanded to do. There's nothing wrong with wanting to impact those around you for the Lord. But we must not only pour out. All of our focus and planting must not all be outward or centered around numbers. We must never forget our own soul salvation in all our outward works for others.

Paul reminds the Ephesians to take heed to themselves when they attempt to restore a brother who is overtaken in a fault. Paul refers to how he brings his body into subjection so that after having preached the gospel to the saving of many, he himself would not be a castaway (I Cor. 9:27). We are to make sure we cultivate our faith and grow spiritually as well as teaching others or having the outward fruit we want in our lives—careers, spouses, children, finances, influence.

Another reason areas could be barren in your life, the spiritual application of the principle, is God wants to be recognized as God. We see God at work in stories of barrenness in the bible. The bible describes wombs as being shut or opened and makes it clear God is the One who opens and closes wombs. When Rachel tells Jacob, give me children or I'll die, Jacob responds by telling her that he isn't the one who has closed her womb. God does this (Gen.

30:1-2).

What's being shown in many of these cases is the *omnipotence* of God. God is all powerful. He is the one who determines what happens in our lives and what doesn't happen in our lives despite our desires and wants.

We can see He wants to give us good things. Nearly every woman in the bible who is described as barren eventually has a child. Their barrenness is not forever but for a season. There is a purpose for this barrenness. A woman giving birth after a lifetime of barrenness outside of childbearing years proves God is at work and in control.

Have you ever thought maybe you have areas of lack in your life to give God an opportunity to show Himself as God in an amazing way? It all leads back to Him and His glory. Anything we give to God will grow, but we aren't able to determine its growth or the timetable by which it grows.

Maybe you'll wait longer than you want to before you have a husband, but maybe God is showing you He is your husband. All the things you are looking for in a husband, God is already giving you: love, provision, a best friend, someone who listens to you, etc.

Not only might God be revealing His nature and our need for Him, maybe He's about to reveal His power by giving us a crop beyond what we ever could have imagined in this area.

The question is are you letting lack and barrenness do what it's supposed to do in your life? Are you drawing near to God? Are you laying your burdens and desires at His feet? Are you allowing His grace to be sufficient?

That last one is a killer, isn't it? What if God's grace was sufficient for us? What if God's unmerited favor was enough? What if we realize all good and perfect gifts come from God, including the ability to deal with and do all the unpleasant things in life?

If God never heals areas of barrenness in our lives, is His grace enough? Will we still wait with expectation on Him or will we start striving on our own?

God's grace isn't just Him giving us the things we want, it is giving us the ability to endure the unpleasant with the attitude God is still good. What He is doing for me is more than I deserve no matter what He is not doing for me.

What would happen if we understood we could conquer disappointment, doubt, feelings of inadequacy and the lies of the enemy through Christ? What if we allowed "I can do all things" & "we are more than conquerors" to apply to situations where we didn't get what we wanted, in situations where we don't feel good? What if we really learned to be content in every season, wherever we are, with whatever we have?

What if the answer isn't in getting the desires of our heart, but surrendering our heart and desires to God? Didn't God say to seek His kingdom and righteousness? But not to gain food, shelter, clothes, relationships, status, or people. If you seek His kingdom and righteousness and never get anything but His kingdom and righteousness, you are blessed to overflowing!

God, in His mercy and grace, promised we will be taken care of in the most essential ways by seeking Him. But do you want God for Himself or what you think He will do for you? Are you seeking Him and His will to know what to do with what He has given you, or are you only seeking Him to ask for more? What did you come to see?

While we may give God our areas of barrenness and lack and allow Him to use them in our lives to His glory, we must also be mindful of the fact producing fruit is a commandment. When God created the earth, He said let the earth bring forth grass, the herb yielding seed, and the fruit tree yielding fruit after his kind, whose seed is in itself, upon the earth; and it was so (Gen. 1:11). God saw this as good. God commanded the animals to be fruitful and multiply after their kind (Gen. 1:22) and saw this as good. He commanded the man and woman He made to be fruitful and multiply also (Gen. 1:28).

This is not only a law of nature in a physical sense but in a spiritual sense as well. God commanded us to be fruitful. Jesus describes Himself as the true vine in John 15. As a branch can't produce fruit of itself except it is in the vine, we can't bear fruit unless we abide in Christ (v. 4). Any branch not bearing fruit is taken away (v. 2) and every branch not connected to the vine withers away. Both are gathered up, cast into the fire and burned (v. 6). We are reassured if we abide in Christ and let Him abide in us, we will bring forth much fruit (v. 5).

The Spirit produces fruit. The evidence of the indwelling of the Holy Spirit is you bear the fruit of His seed. There may be some areas where God has allowed us to experience barrenness to show us our need for Him, but those places, once we have given them to God, will also produce fruit. The fruit is God being glorified, the fruit produced by abiding in the Lord, the fruit of the Spirit.

Some of us aren't barren, however. Some of us aren't bare and will bring forth fruit in our season. Some of us are unfruitful. The problem isn't we aren't able to bear fruit. We can produce fruit, but we refuse to. There are several illustrations given in the bible of unfruitfulness pertinent to this discussion.

1. Onan spilled his seed because **he knew it would be credited to someone else.** Onan knew if he had a child with Tamar, the child would be his brother's child. He would be fulfilling his duty to his brother's lineage and not his own. Onan didn't want to do this, so he spilled his seed and was smote by God for it.

   Matthew 5:16 says men should see our good works and glorify God (our Father) in Heaven. Some of us don't want that. We want the recognition, the credit. So we withhold our gifts because we won't be lauded for them.

2. In the parable of the talents, the servant who received one talent buried his in the earth. When asked why he didn't give his master back more than he received, he explained he was afraid to lose what he had been given, so he buried it. The master took what he had and gave it away.

   Some of us are **afraid we will lose what little we have if we try to grow.** We hide our light under a bushel or bury what God has given us because we don't know if we can maximize it or give more back than we received. But God multiplies whatever we give Him. It's a principle shown over and over again in the bible. You can't lose by using your talents and abilities for the Lord; you can only be more fruitful. (The Parable of the Talents Matt 25:14-30).

3. Jesus comes across a fig tree on one of his journeys which looks good for fruit, but when He reaches it, it has no figs on it. Jesus curses the fig tree for its unfruitfulness. Later, when they pass this fig tree again, they see it withered.
Sometimes **we cultivate the appearance but aren't producing fruit (Mk. 11:12-14, 20).** Like the fig tree, we have big beautiful leaves and the appearance of growing, but no fruit. We are so busy looking busy we aren't doing anything. We go to church every Sunday, we post to Instagram, Facebook and Snap Chat about studying the bible, and we wear all the t-shirts with the biblical sayings and sentiments, but when we are tested, we have no fruits of the spirit to sustain us.

4. When Mordecai comes to Esther and requests she go to the king and ask him to spare the Jews, she is conflicted. She doesn't want to put herself in the line of fire to save the people. Mordecai tells her if she doesn't do this, someone else will be raised up to do it. But she will have missed out (Esth. 4:14). We can get beside ourselves and **believe if we don't do something it won't be done**. We want to show how important we are. We will refuse to work or participate to punish those who don't recognize our value. If God wants something to go forward, it's going forward with or without you. Those who are serious about God recognize the focus is on God and not themselves. They seek for God's will to be done and not their own.

5. When God told Jonah to go to Ninevah, Jonah

decided to get on a ship to Tarshish instead (Jon. 1:3). Jonah didn't want to go to Ninevah because he knew if the people repented, God's wrath would be turned away from them (Jon. 4:1-2). He didn't want them to be saved. He ran away to thwart the will of God.

Sometimes **we don't want to yield a particular kind of fruit**. We run from the refining process because we don't want to forgive someone who has wronged us, or we don't want to accept we aren't meant to be in a certain position. Maybe I don't want to deal with situations designed to grow my patience. Maybe I don't care a certain man isn't God's best for me. Why can't I do one thing I want to do without God messing it up?

We fail to realize God does everything for our good. He isn't trying to rob us of something wonderful but save us from sin and death. Beyond this, God's will is going to be done no matter what I want to happen. It's not dependent on me getting with the program. I may miss God's blessings in my life because of my disobedience, but His plans will come to fruition with or without my participation.

There is a season to everything. If you aren't bearing fruit in an area, maybe it's not the season for bearing fruit in that area. Maybe you are bare for a season in some things. Perhaps you are barren in an area and need to surrender it to God and seek His will regarding the area. But take some time to examine yourself and evaluate if you might be the reason you are unfruitful. Have you surrendered to God? Have you stayed where God planted you or have you uprooted yourself and fled from His face?

CHAPTER SEVEN

> ¹³This is why I speak to them in parables: Though seeing, they do not see; though hearing, they do not hear or understand. ¹⁴In them is fulfilled the prophecy of Isaiah: You will be ever hearing but never understanding; you will be ever seeing but never perceiving. ¹⁵For this people's heart has become calloused; they hardly hear with their ears, and they have closed their eyes. Otherwise they might see with their eyes, hear with their ears, understand with their hearts and turn, and I would heal them. ¹⁶But blessed are your eyes because they see, and your ears because they hear. Matt 13:13-16

Our faith controls our senses. It rules our perception, determining what we hear and what we see. It limits what we say. Faith is an essential element of growth. But the growth spurred by faith is often limited by doubt, fear, sin, selfish pursuit of money, recognition, and the fulfillment of our lusts.

Many limitations on growing closer to Christ stem from impairments to our faith. Being spiritually deaf, dumb, and/or blind limit our knowledge and experiences with Christ. This limitation keeps our faith, and our relationship with Christ, from growing. We must be healed from these conditions to experience true growth.

How do we know if we are spiritually deaf, dumb or blind? What are the symptoms? How are these ailments dealt with in scripture? How do you treat them?

Selective Hearing

⁸Though he were a Son, yet learned he obedience by the things which he suffered; ⁹And being made perfect, he became the author of eternal salvation unto all them that obey him; ¹⁰Called of God a high priest after the order of Melchisedec. ¹¹Of whom we have many things to say, and hard to be uttered, seeing ye are dull of hearing. ¹²For when for the time ye ought to be teachers, ye have need that one teach you again which *be* the first principles of the oracles of God; and are become such as have need of milk, and not of strong meat. ¹³For every one that useth milk *is* unskillful in the word of righteousness: for he is a babe. ¹⁴But strong meat belongeth to them that are of full age, *even* those who by reason of use have their senses exercised to discern both good and evil. Heb. 5:8-14

The first ailment we will explore is deafness. In the above passage we see one of the spiritual attributes of being dull of hearing or spiritually deaf is immaturity. Someone who is spiritually immature is like a child sticking his fingers in his ears and chanting "na na na na nah! I can't hear you!"

Other translations translate dull of hearing as no longer trying to understand (NIV) and dull and sluggish in your spiritual hearing and disinclined to listen (AMP). The spiritually deaf person only hears what they want to hear. Their comprehension of what they hear with spiritual ears is low, and application is non-existent. They can't remember the basics, let alone go to the next level.

Hearing is the first step of faith. Faith comes by hearing, and hearing the word of God (Rom. 10:17). If you can't hear, you can't believe. If you can't believe, it is impossible to please God (Heb. 11:6).

Hearing loss is one of the first signs of spiritual death. Hearing is essential to our growth beyond the point of obedience to the gospel. We have to keep learning if we are going to improve. Moreover, as the bible says, if we stop listening to instruction, we will stray from the words of knowledge (Prov. 19:27). Not only is hearing essential for growth; it's essential for maintaining the knowledge we already have.

Moses is a classic example of spiritual deafness. When God calls Moses and sends him to tell Pharaoh to let the people go, Moses suffers from selective hearing. When Moses tells Pharaoh what the Lord said, Pharaoh makes the people's work harder. The people become discouraged and disappointed. But this is because Moses didn't give them all the information God had given him.

Moses was told Pharaoh would not let the people go into the wilderness to praise God. God would have to deliver the people with a mighty hand (Ex. 3:19-20). It's already been foretold Moses would go and the results wouldn't be favorable. God needed to deliver them with a mighty hand because He was bringing judgment on Egypt. Yet all Moses seems to hear and translate to the people is "God is going to deliver you." He only gives them part of the message. He doesn't express an understanding of the full message.

After the people are given more work and reject him, Moses goes back to God. He's upset and discouraged. God tells Moses exactly what He told him before. Why didn't Moses hear the Lord the first time?

Moses wanted to be liked and accepted. He wanted the people to be behind him in his efforts. Wanting the people's approval, He only shares with them the good news.

Sometimes we can be guilty of doing the same thing. We tell people to come to the Lord and have their sins washed away. We tell them they will have a home in Heaven. But we forget to tell them what happens in between baptism and Heaven. Before you get to Heaven, you're going to have to live in obedience to God's word. There's going to be persecution, false accusations, and self- denial. Being set apart from this world is going to feel lonely and isolating sometimes. It may make you feel as if you aren't enough. There will be times you want to quit. It's not going to be easy.

Sometimes we don't convey the requirements of

Christianity because we want people to come to Christ. We only share the positives. We even do this to one another. We encourage each other with the "good" scriptures and gloss over people's issues, hardships, and trials. We refuse to hear what they are saying because if we hear it, we have to respond to their needs, and we don't feel capable of doing so.

We do people a disservice when we only hear what we want to hear in the bible. The word of God addresses the needs of the people of God. By pretending we don't have needs, we miss the blessing of God's solutions for our problems. When we don't hear God, we can't understand what He wants us to do.

We must desire the word so we can grow by it (I Pet. 2:2).

David says God spoke once and twice I have heard this (Psalm 62:11). It's amazing how things can come back to us, how we can hear something one time and not really understand it, then hear it again and it makes perfect sense. It's said in the right situation. We completely get exactly what's going on.

It's important to intently study the word because every time you look at it, you're going to get more out of it. The more you read it and the deeper you dig into it, the more you discover God's word is regenerative in a way nothing else we can read is. There's always something new to get out of it. There's always something directly applicable to where you are at this stage of life right now.

But if we are dull of hearing, only listening to the parts we think sound good and insistent on being stuck on milk instead of moving on to strong meat, then we are going to miss out on a lot of who God is and growing a deeper relationship with Him. Hearing is our first line of defense against atrophy, neglecting our salvation and being caught unawares when Jesus returns.

Another example of someone with a hearing problem is Balaam. Balaam proclaims "I can only say what God told me to say (Num. 22:18)." Balaam asks God what he should do when Balak sends men with a request for Balaam to curse the Israelites. God tells Balaam not to go with these men, and Balaam explains this to the men (Num. 22:12). He seems to have heard correctly. But when Balak sends men of a higher position of influence who offer more money, Balaam asks God a second time whether or not he should go with these men (Num. 22:15-19). Why?

Perhaps he questioned if he heard God correctly. Did God really say not to go with them? He wants to hear he can go and collect the money and other items on offer, but this isn't what God told him. This time, God tells Balaam to go, but God isn't happy with Balaam and sends an angel to kill him.

Sometimes God gives people over to their lusts, as Paul says in Romans (Rom. 1:28). This means they don't have a conscience. They aren't hearing anything contrary to what they want to do or believe. They are not pricked.

This condition is evident in the world, and unfortunately in members of the church, today. People work hard to shut down any voice opposed to what they want to do, how they want to live, and what they deem acceptable. Not only are they not effected by the truth, they don't want others to hear it. They seek to silence the truth.

It is our job as obedient children of God to share the truth no matter the opposition. People need to hear the word of the Lord in order to be saved. We can't let spiritual deafness rob us of the opportunity to lead someone to salvation.

Closed Mouths

Another spiritual ailment is dumbness, or muteness. There are a few different causes of dumbness in the bible. Not all of them are bad. Indeed, Jesus didn't open His mouth when He was taken and sentenced to crucifixion. Jesus taught against praying with vain repetitions, thinking we would be heard by our many words. Solomon, in the above passage from Ecclesiastes exhorted people to realize their relationship with God and to let their words be few.

Even though dumbness can be an attribute, there are

instances in which it is characteristic of a spiritual ailment. We see dumbness in the bible brought about by demons possessing people. We also see God closing and opening mouths to accomplish His purposes.

One example of God shutting someone's mouth is found in Luke 1. Zechariah, the father of John the Baptist, is struck dumb after the angel Gabriel visits him to announce Zechariah's wife will give birth to the forerunner of the Messiah. Gabriel tells Zechariah his son will turn the people back to God and prepare the way for the Messiah. Zechariah questions Gabriel's pronouncements. He is skeptical. He asks "how can I know what you're saying is true?"

Gabriel closes Zechariah's mouth. Gabriel tells Zechariah he won't speak again until the things Gabriel told him come to pass. This is done so Zechariah can believe.

Zechariah doesn't say another word until after the birth of John. When people question why Elizabeth named the baby John and not Zechariah, Zechariah writes on a tablet "His name is John," and his mouth is opened. He begins to praise God and prophesy about who John is going to be.

God closes mouths. And he opens them. There are some things we need to remain silent on. When we hear from the Lord, do we, like Zechariah, question the word? Does God have to prove to us the truth of His word?

Discernment is necessary to determine when we need to keep silent and when we are afflicted with spiritual dumbness. When Jesus was crucified, He didn't answer the accusations against Him. As a sheep is dumb before the shearers, Jesus opened not His mouth (Isa. 53:7-8; Matt. 26:62-63). He had spent three years proclaiming who He was through word and deed. When He was put on trial, He didn't have to say anything. He knew God's will was being done and He was submitted to it.

What Jesus did was not spiritual dumbness. Zechariah's mouth being closed is not the spiritual dumbness I'm exhorting you to fight in order to grow in your relationship with Christ. The spiritual dumbness we must fight against is the urge to keep our mouths closed when we should be speaking up. It's giving God excuses why we can't speak to someone to the saving of their soul. It's when we refuse to say what God places on our heart to say to encourage another Christian. It's when we through word or deed tell God to send someone else because we can't speak.

Another example of this is Balaam's donkey. This animal sees things Balaam cannot. The donkey sees the angel of the Lord sent to oppose and kill Balaam. She's beaten three times for saving his life and she's not able to say anything. Then God opens her mouth and she is able to question Balaam and speak to him.

This is a powerful illustration. There are times when God opens people's mouths and really speaks through them to reveal what His will is. This is the other side of being dumb, when God has placed something in you to say. He takes over talking for them or He puts His words physically in their mouths. No matter how you try, it's like fire in your bones. You have to let it out. You can't sit on it. You can try not to say it, but you have to.

One of the things I like about the story of Jeremiah is his boldness. Jeremiah is referred to as the weeping prophet. He wrote the book on lamenting. He's always railing. He doesn't have the flowery language David or Isaiah have. He tells it like it is and the people didn't like his messages.

But God says to Jeremiah "I knew you before you were formed in your mother's womb (Jer. 1:5)." Sometimes we take comfort in this without realizing the full import of what God is saying. God is saying He knows the personality Jeremiah has before He calls him. He knows Jeremiah is young, brash and bold. He knows Jeremiah feels unqualified. He knows Jeremiah has a problem with his mouth. He knows Jeremiah wants to say things the right way, to persuade people instead of beat them over the head. God tells him, I already know all about you. I know how you are. There's a reason I'm choosing you to say this.

God knows our abilities. He knows our limitations. When He calls us to say something, He didn't forget who we are or what we've done. He didn't make a mistake. He meant to call us. He wanted us to speak.

God equips us in our experiences in life, in our personalities, in ways we can't even fathom to go to certain people and speak to them in an encouraging, uplifting way to bring them to salvation. Our willingness to speak up can alter lives in one significant moment or change their course forever. This only happens when we give God the power over our speech.

God knows if we can speak to people, we can change them. We can become cohesive. When we are on one accord, there is nothing we can't do through the power of Christ. When the people are building the Tower of Babel, God confounds their languages because once the people get on one accord and work together like this, there will be nothing beyond them to do (Gen. 11:6).

If you can't effectively communicate, you might as well be dumb. This is an encouragement for us because there are some people we can't speak to. Maybe we feel silenced by circumstances, situations or people. Maybe we feel silenced by God. He doesn't want us to say certain things to people. If our Gospel be hid, it is hid from unbelievers (II Cor. 4:3). The wisdom of God is foolishness to man (I Cor. 3:19) and vice versa. We can't communicate with people who are in the world. God's wisdom is foolishness to this world. It doesn't make any sense.

> If the blind lead the blind, they both will fall in the ditch. (Matt. 15:14)

It's amazing how many people in the Bible are said to be blind, either physically or spiritually. Many of Jesus' miracles involved giving sight to the blind. Jesus also called the scribes and Pharisees blind on several occasions. The bible invites us to see and hear and calls those who see and hear blessed. It's impossible to grow close to Christ if we are spiritually blind.

Blindness, spiritual or physical, is the inability to see or process/interpret sensory details received through the eyes. Someone who is blind is unaware of their surroundings and unable to make decisions about which way to go based on what can be seen. They have no special recognition of what's around or in front of them. They are unable to see dangers.

The bible says "we wrestle not against flesh and blood but against principalities, against powers, against the rulers of the darkness of this world, against spiritual wickedness in high places (Eph. 6:12)." You can't see spiritual wickedness with physical eyes. It takes spiritual sight to see the spiritual wickedness behind the person or circumstances we see with our physical eyes.

Just as it takes spiritual sight to see spiritual wickedness, it takes spiritual sight to see God at work in the midst of situations. When an army surrounds the city where Elisha and his servant are, the servant is worried. Elisha prays for his servants' eyes to be opened. When the servant's eyes are opened, he sees the army of God surrounding the physical army encamped outside the city. In this instance, not only does God give the servant spiritual sight, he takes the physical sight of the army and sends them back where they came from.

Sight is an important element of our Christian journey. Sometimes we downplay sight when we don't understand the role of sight in faith. We walk by faith and not by sight (2 Cor. 5:7); this is true. People say "well the bible says, 'faith is the substance of things hoped for, the evidence of things not seen (Heb. 11:1)." Again, this is true. Faith *is* the evidence of things not seen, but this doesn't mean we will never see things by faith.

We're to look for the coming of the Lord. We are to see and interpret the signs around us. The bible says to watch and pray. It tells us to exhort each other all the more as we see the day approaching.

Sight is very important. But what are you seeing? This is where we get hung up. People who are blinded by the things of this world don't see things spiritually. The gospel is eye opening. Yes, there are things we must choose to believe God for even when we don't see anything to inspire such belief, but the exhortation to watch for, look for or seek after is seen throughout scripture. We see where God tells us what to look for. But if we refuse to see, if we follow the wrong people, and if we insist on being in darkness, we won't be able to see.

"We walk by faith and not by sight" does not mean we stumble around in the dark stubbing our toes on the unseen obstacles of life. Sight requires light. Guess what God is? God is light and in Him there is no darkness (I John 1:5). If we walk in the light as He is in the light, we have fellowship one with another (I John 1:7). Following God and His word, we won't fall into every dip, depression or ditch on the road of life.

Having sight is to have knowledge or be able to see what is happening around you and make decisions based on what you see. Faith is the light or sight aid by which we see and interact with the world. Faith is not blindness; it is a flood of light.

We know who we are, whose we are, what we're supposed to do and where we are going. This light is essential for growth, like sunshine to plants.

If you can't see—"I can't see how I'm going to get over this." "I can't see how I'm going to do this"--it's because you don't have light. You're operating outside of Christ and in your own will. You're operating outside of reading the word. Or you're reading it and not studying, understanding, rightly dividing it, or applying it. There's consistent imagery of God being light or light coming from God. Something about your relationship with Christ, your communication with Him, is out of balance when you can't see or recognize the path you're on.

People are very definitive who recognize Jesus and proclaim Him. John sees Him and says "Behold! The Lamb of God who taketh away the sins of the world (John 1:29)." No question. I know who He is.

When we can't see, we question. Sometimes we're not really blind; we're discouraged. We are beat down. We have the belief kicked out of us. The same John who said "behold the Lamb of God that taketh away the sins of the world" is also the one who sent messengers to Christ when he was in prison to ask "art thou the Christ or should we look for another (Lk. 7:19; Matt 11:2-3)?" John had gotten to a point where he was so depressed and dejected he was no longer sure of what he used to know assuredly. There are people who we come into contact with who are this kind of blind.

Whatever kind of spiritual blindness we have, the cure is the same: a) obedience to the gospel, b) repentance and confession, and c) studying God's word. God's word is where His plans are revealed. It is likened to all sources of light which drive out the darkness which can hinder our sight. When it's dark and you can't see things clearly, the word of God is described as a lamp and a light (Ps. 119:105). Christ Himself is described as the light of the world (John 8:12), who shines in the darkness (John 1:4-5). If you aren't able to see things spiritually, get close to the Light.

It is essential for us to be able to hear, specifically to hear the word of God, to be open to it. To be receptive to it. To allow it to pierce us, change us, cut out things which shouldn't be in us. We cannot let ourselves get dull of hearing.

Sometimes you don't need to be able to speak. I know from the example of scripture several times over--with Balaam's donkey, with Balaam himself, with Jeremiah, with Isaiah, with Zechariah father of John the Baptist, with the disciples on the Day of Pentecost and with so many others--when it is time for us to speak, God will endow us with the ability to speak and to speak His word.

The cure for spiritual blindness is to be obedient to the Lord's word, to repent, confess and return to Him when we fall short, and to study His word.

At each stage, studying God's word is vital.

CHAPTER EIGHT

Taste & See

> O taste and see that the Lord is good: blessed is the man that trusteth in him. Ps. 34:8

The more we understand who God is and what He does, the better relationship we can have with Him. We see over and over again in God's word how He has responded to His people in their waywardness. We see many examples of God dealing with those who are spiritually deaf, dumb and blind. We can better understand how God deals with us if we understand who He is and what He expects in order to be in relationship with us.

God hears us. God states explicitly several times He heard someone. When God calls Moses to lead the people out of Egypt, God tells Moses to let the people know God saw and heard them (Ex. 3:7). We know God hears His people. There are occasions when God does not hear, however, not because He is deaf, but because He will not associate with sin. God is willing to hear us. Even if we put ourselves in a position where he does not hear us, He has avenues by which He can hear us again:

> If my people, which are called by my name, shall humble themselves, and pray, and seek my face, and turn from their wicked ways; then I will hear from heaven, and will forgive their sin, and will heal their land. (II Chr. 7:14)

God is not the one with the hearing problem: we are.

God exhorts His people to hear Him consistently throughout scripture. Hearing is essential to cultivating faith and building a relationship. If we feel God isn't hearing us, we must take an honest look at our lives to determine whether we are in a position to be heard by God. We must adjust ourselves in relationship to God, not the other way around. When we draw near to God, God will draw near to us (Jas. 4:8). We must decide to be near Him.

If we feel like we aren't hearing from God, again, we need to evaluate ourselves. Am I in the audience to hear from God? Am I opening His word, through which He speaks to me? Am I attending worship service to hear His word preached? Am I attending bible study to study His word in fellowship with other believers?

The second thing to ask yourself is if God has answered you and you are ignoring the answer because you want a different one. In this more obsessed culture, it's easy to ignore God's "no" and keep asking God for an answer.

The third thing we need to evaluate if we feel like we aren't hearing from God is the possibility God is silent for a reason. God moves in the fullness of time, in due season—in other words, when things are supposed to happen. It's not up to us to determine when God will answer us anymore than it's up to us to qualify how the Lord will answer.

If we have a hearing problem, we must treat our dull hearing with the sharp word of God. When the disciples were trying to go ahead of God and make plans to build three tabernacles after they'd witnessed the transfiguration, God said, "This is my beloved Son, in whom I am well pleased; hear ye him (Matt. 17:5)." The same exhortation is given to us today. We must hear Jesus. Jesus says His sheep know His voice. We shouldn't move or act on any other voice or follow any other advice.

If you feel like God is being silent, then wait until you hear His voice! If you asked God if you should leave your job and you didn't hear anything from Him, go to work on time, do your job and represent Him there until you *do* hear from Him. It is always better to wait on the Lord than to move outside of his will.

God is always speaking to us. In fact it says explicitly in Hebrews 1:1-2 God has spoken to us by the prophets and now speaks through His son, Jesus. Even though He's told us the end of the story, He's still speaking to us through His word today.

God has not been struck dumb. He hasn't decided not to talk to us anymore. God speaks to us and through us in a variety of ways. He has been known to open mouths and speak through people. He does this today through ministers, elders, and people in our lives. The person doesn't even have to be a Christian to be used by God to speak to you.

In the person of Jesus, we see silence used as a fulfillment of prophecy, but also as a lesson for us. Every criticism doesn't need an answer. The only answer Jesus gives is to whether or not He is the son of God. How much better would our lives be if we would live as if the only accusation we needed to answer was that of being a child of God? If we didn't use our ability to speak to cut down every critique or every person who crossed our path? If we didn't use it to bite and consume each other?

Being dumb is not always a bad thing. But there are times we must be able to give an answer or make a confession or profession of faith. We need to be able to speak boldly at these times. We must set a guard over the gates of our mouths and watch the words we let out into the world. The word is so important and integral in the salvation process. We often quote the scripture that faith comes by hearing and hearing the word of God, but we forget people can't believe in something they haven't heard. How can people hear the word of God if we aren't speaking it? God continues to speak to us today through His Son because He is still saving people today. He calls us to speak to those lost in sin as well as to speak encouragement to one another.

God is a god who sees us. Hagar calls God "The God Who Sees." This is just as true today as it was in her day. God sees what we do in secret and He rewards openly. In the book of Hebrews we learn all things are naked and opened unto the eyes of him with whom we have to do (Heb. 4:13).

God blinds. The men in Sodom and Gomorrah were blinded when they attempted to force their way into Lot's house in their lusts to have the "men" who were visiting Lot (Gen. 19:11). God blinded the eyes of the army encamped around Elisha and the children of Israel (2 Kgs. 6:18).

But God also opens eyes. He opened Balaam's eyes to the angel that stood in the road to oppose him (Num. 22:31). He opened the eyes of Elisha's assistant to see Heaven's army around the army that surrounded them (2 Kgs. 6:17). He gives the children of Israel the opportunity to see when He sent the spies from Kadesh Barnea into the land of Canaan. Indeed, just as in all the previous categories, Jesus healed blindness.

But we have a responsibility with the sight God gives us. We choose what we will focus on. We decide what things we see are the most important. The spies who went into Canaan all saw the same things, but ten put more importance on the size of the inhabitants of the land than they did on the land being everything God promised them it would be. If the land is what God promised, why wouldn't they believe in His other promises? Had God failed them at any point? Yet they were constantly being hampered instead of helped by what they could see.

Here's another point to consider: just as God can blind someone the devil blinds as well. The god of this world, the devil, blinds men's eyes so they can't see the light of the gospel (2 Cor. 4:4). We must be cognizant of the devil's ability to blind and seek the illumination of the light of God in every situation.

These characteristics show we have a God who has not turned away from us. He hears us. He sees us. He is concerned about us. He remembers His promises to us. Beyond how we can prevent ourselves from becoming deaf, dumb and blind and how we can be healed from these spiritual ailments, we must know God is none of these things.

God is always greater. God has this ability we don't have. Nothing is impossible for God. There are things we can't see or hear coming. There are things we are unaware of. There are things we can't say. We can't pronounce a binding judgment on anyone or add to or take away from God's word without repercussion. But God knows all. There's nothing impossible for God to do, and there's nothing impossible for us to do if we are operating in relationship with Him, desiring what He desires for us. Operating in His will and doing what he has called us to do.

We must be on the lookout in our lives for spiritual deafness, dumbness, and blindness. Those who don't hear with their ears or see with their eyes can't understand with their hearts and come to the one who can heal them of all their infirmities. Spiritual immaturity, a weak foundation of faith, a refusal to hear God's word and obey it, and sin all contribute to a loss of our spiritual senses. We must not let these muscles atrophy but must exercise them by reason of use.

We must take any ailments to the Great Physician in these areas. We cannot let the devil possess us, blind us, bind us, or otherwise cause us to miss the salvation and freedom God gives to all those who obey Him.

Are you spiritually deaf, dumb or blind? Get it right, right now. Read the word to hear from God. Decide to wait on Him and His will as long as it takes. Strengthen your faith so you can walk by its light and see the path before you. Don't allow the devil to blind you and keep you from seeing the light of the gospel.

Be ready to give an answer in season and out of season for your faith, but don't answer fools in their folly or be pulled into useless arguments. Set a guard over your mouth so what comes out of it will not defile you.

God has the cure for what ails you, sisters. You only need to ask.

How many examples of people asking in faith and being healed by God do we need to see and hear before we believe He will do the same for us? Nothing has overtaken us uncommon to mankind. No temptation has befallen us Christ didn't overcome.

We don't have to turn a blind eye or a deaf ear to God because we don't believe we can live up to the things He requires. God is faithful to complete the work He began in you! He is the one who gave you the desire to seek His righteousness, and He will be the one that works in you to accomplish the goal of salvation if you believe in Him!

CHAPTER NINE

Just a Touch

For we have not an high priest which cannot be touched with the feeling of our infirmities; but was in all points tempted like as we are, yet without sin. Heb. 4:15

Touch is essential to growth. Studies have shown the lack of caring and nurturing touches in newborn babies reduces their IQ, increases the risk of behavioral and psychological problems, profoundly affects their immune systems and can lead to death. A baby's brain expects constant physical touch and does not grow without it.[3]

Not only does touch effect the brain, it also effects physical growth. Even if you feed and otherwise care for an infant, the absence of physical touch slows their growth and even causes them to die.

Touch is not only essential for infants, however. Studies have shown we communicate more accurately through touch than any other non-verbal form of communication.[4]

The emotional and social components of touch are inseparable from the physical. In other words, we react to

---

[3] http://www.huffingtonpost.com/maia-szalavitz/how-orphanages-kill-babie_b_549608.html

[4] https://www.psychologytoday.com/articles/201303/the-power-touch

touch differently based on who we think is touching us and in what situation we are being touched.

Touch communicates sympathy, empathy, anger, desire, love, affection, caring, and fellowship. It effects how teams work together and how humans relate to one another in work environments and families.

Why am I taking the time to tell you all of this?

We can't talk about spiritual deficiencies and not talk about an inability to touch and be touched. As essential as physical touch is to physical growth and the establishment of physical bonds, the ability to touch and be touched spiritually is even more essential. When we don't have spiritual contact with God and other Christians, we don't grow; we die. If we are going to be serious about growth, we have to understand the importance of touch in our spiritual lives and cultivate a culture of constant spiritual contact in our churches.

What is touch? How is it used in the bible?

The essential meaning of the word translated as touch is to physically contact something or someone. Touching is close personal contact. In Hebrews 4:15, the word translated as touch means to sympathize with, to be compassionate, or to have compassion upon. Words translated as touch in the bible can also mean to reach or cause to reach, to be struck down with disease, or to inflict plagues. The touch of God is always authoritative. It's sometimes official, enabling someone to serve (Is. 6:7; Jer. 1:9; Dan. 10:16). No matter the usage, touch in the bible effects change.

When the devil presents himself before God with the sons of God in the book of Job, he tells God that if He will put forth his hand and touch all that Job has, touch his bone and his flesh, that Job will curse Him to His face (Job 1:11, 2:5). This means God has control of what comes into the lives of His people. Satan is not able to touch Job without God's permission, and what He can do when He touches God's people is limited by God. God tells the devil he cannot touch Job, and later when He gives the devil permission to touch Job, God tells the devil he must spare

Job's life (Job 1:12, 2:6).

If something evil or bad has touched your life, it is not that it slipped past God. The things that are allowed to touch us are moderated and regulated by God and there is a purpose to us being touched. If we feel pulled to do something good to touch someone else's life, the desire came from the Lord.

In the same way Satan sought God's permission to touch Job and tempt him to curse the Lord to His face, the devil also tempted our Lord and Savior Jesus Christ in the wilderness after He was baptized in obedience to the will of His Father. The lust of the flesh, the lust of the eye and the pride of life were all put before Jesus, and He chose not to pursue them. The same ways in which the devil tempts us, he tempted Christ.

But let's pause for a moment and consider what this incident says to us about temptation and being touched. Jesus had been in the synagogues astonishing those who heard Him as a child, growing in wisdom and stature and in favor with God and man. But it wasn't until Jesus was baptized by John and the Spirit of God led Him into the wilderness He was tempted of the devil.

We can do any good deeds we want. We can impress all manner of people with our understanding and wisdom beyond our years. We can acquire whatever accolades we want and seem to go from strength to strength with no problems. It is only when we are obedient to the gospel call that Satan seeks to touch us. It is then the devil wants to put forth his hand and turn our joy into mourning.

The devil doesn't need to touch you if you aren't living for God or trying to be obedient to Him. It's not about being a good person; it's about being a child of God, born into the family of God by the water and the spirit, purchased by the blood of Jesus, partakers of the inheritance of the saints in light: these are the people the devil seeks to devour.

Throughout His life, Jesus displayed an ability to be touched and a propensity to touch. The bible says Jesus had compassion for several of the people He healed or whose loved ones He resurrected. He weeps. He gets upset with how people who are gambling in the temple. He experiences fatigue and rejection. He takes part in celebrations like weddings and feasts. Jesus had a life while He was on earth like we do with all the attendant joys, trials, and tribulations. The bible tells us these things so we know He can sympathize with us.

In the beginning of this chapter, I gave facts about physical touch which I believe apply to our spiritual lives:

- Touch is essential for growth. It activates chemical processes and cells in the body to grow. When we are touched by what's going on around us as a body, it should activate us. We should start growing and arranging ourselves in response to the need. A church with members who are unable to be touched is dead or dying. A person who is no longer able to empathize and sympathize with others is spiritually dead.
- Touching is the most accurate form of nonverbal communication. If you are not touching or being touched, you are not accurately interpreting what someone is trying to communicate to you. You aren't able to translate their needs or serve them well.
- The emotional and social components of touch are inseparable from the physical. People we have an emotional and social connection with are better able to touch us and we are more likely to touch them. We will accept certain touches from someone close to us which would be inappropriate and unwanted from a stranger. We must be in touch with people in order to touch them. We must have an established relationship to avoid misunderstanding of our efforts to touch others.

There's more to say about the role of touching in our Christian journey, but it will be addressed in a later chapter.

Right now, let's focus on two questions:
1. Christ touched because He could be touched. He could both empathize and sympathize with our feelings. He wasn't harsh or cold. He didn't take a position of not understanding why we couldn't get it right or being unsympathetic to our suffering the consequences of our choices. Can you be touched? Or are you too busy shaking your head and deploring the youth of today? Are you ignoring the touch you feel because you have judged someone unworthy of your sympathy? Have you lost your sensitivity and your ability to be touched by what's happening in someone else's life?
2. If you are able to be touched and have compassion for people, are you touching them in response to being touched? One of the definitions of touch is to reach or cause to reach. Christ and later His disciples healed through touch. They reached out and took people's hand to pull them out of their afflictions. Who have you reached and touched lately? Whose hand have you grabbed hold of? Who has reached out to you and gained strength and healing?

CHAPTER TEN

Spiritual Alzheimer's

In my early twenties, I worked at a group home for the developmentally disabled. I performed a series of jobs there, everything from technical assistant to activities coordinator, but what I did most frequently was the afternoon shift. During this shift, I assisted the residents with normal activities like meals as well as worked with them on the goals they chose to work on.

While there, one of my duties was to work with a resident who had Alzheimer's in addition to their developmental disabilities. It was during my work with this resident I learned and experienced firsthand how this disease effects the mind and body.

Although the effect of Alzheimer's on the memory and the tendency of someone with the disease to wander are well-known by those who haven't experienced life with someone suffering from the disease, some of its other characteristics are not. In addition to these symptoms, sufferers also experience insomnia or sleep interruption, paranoia, depression, and mood swings. They can become aggressive and lash out at caregivers. They will even use profanity and exhibit other behaviors uncharacteristic of the person you know them to be. Their moments of lucidity occur for shorter periods of time, with longer stretches between those moments. They revert back to babies before your eyes.

Alzheimer's is a wasting disease. It's degenerative. It ravages a person's mind and body. It robs them of their memories, experiences, assurance, personality, and lives. There is no known cure.

I don't want anyone to think I'm making light of this disease nor the effects it has on those suffering or those caring for the sufferer. I have witnessed the gravity of this disease up close more than once, and probably will again. But its gravity is one of the reasons we study it. We want to find a way to fight this disease. I believe the same gravity needs to be applied to people who are suffering spiritually from attacks that have ravaged them in similar ways.

Our souls are all we have for eternity. We can't afford to let the disease of sin eat away at our soul any more than we can give anything in exchange for it.

There are many in our churches today suffering from spiritual Alzheimer's. Instead of growing in God, they are degenerating. They are falling away. Not only are they falling away, but they are angry and destructive in their leaving, dividing churches, ruining relationships, and fighting those who try to restore them.

The symptoms of spiritual Alzheimer's are just as noticeable and virulent as those of the physical disease. They are characterized by the same behaviors and mental dispositions. Those who suffer from spiritual Alzheimer's tend to do the following:

- **They live in the past.** People with Alzheimer's aren't oriented to time and environment. They often believe they are living during a previous time in their history and expect to be doing things characteristic of that time. Similarly, those with spiritual Alzheimer's focus on things they have done for the Lord in the past. They speak frequently about how involved they used to be or how much they used to give in the collection. They take pride in events and modes of behavior no longer illustrative of their present day realities.
- **They look for dead people or people from their pasts.** People with Alzheimer's

not only live in the past, they expect to see people who were around during that time, many of which have passed on or grown significantly older than they remember. They often mistake caregivers for family members or friends who have passed away or grown up, and they get upset when the caregiver doesn't respond accordingly. Christians suffering with Spiritual Alzheimer's tend to look for people who are dead. They look for people who have been buried with Christ in baptism. They expect repentant people who have been forgiven to still persist in their sinful nature. They don't recognize these people as the new creatures they have become. They still want to treat them as if they are the same person. They tell church members, visitors, and guests about how this person used to be. They refuse to relinquish the person of the past and embrace who the person is now in Christ.

- **They forget.** Forgetfulness is one of the first warning signs of Alzheimer's. Progressive memory loss is the most familiar characteristic of the disease. Caretakers have to constantly remind the individual of pertinent facts or repeat the same information.

  If you are suffering from Spiritual Alzheimer's, you are forgetting things you need to remember. You need to be reminded of them every day. Throughout the Old Testament, God continually commands the children of Israel to remember the things He did for them. There are several retellings of the children of Israel's deliverance from Egypt and their time in the wilderness. There are numerous instances of recounting the law God gave to them. God has them make monuments future generations can see and ask about which will give them an opportunity to share the stories of what God did with their children.

The Bible says these things were written for our learning. It shows us God wants us to remember what He did for us. Paul says before the foundation of the world, the plan for man's salvation was in the mind of God (I Pet. 1:20; Rom. 16:25-26). God commended His love toward us and while we were yet sinners, Christ died for us (Rom 5:8). Christ's death on the cross gave us the opportunity to be saved. Anyone who is baptized into Christ has put on Christ (Gal. 3:27). God has given them His Holy Spirit to dwell within them. All that will live godly must suffer persecution (2 Tim. 3:12). Only those that endure receive a crown (I 9:24-25). These are the things we know. These are the things we must keep on knowing. We must write these truths on our hearts, bind them about our neck, speak them to each other in psalms and hymns and spiritual songs, and go into the world and teach them to others. We must remember God loves us and His love for us is active. He did something for us we could never do for ourselves. He requires of us only things beneficial to us. He is longsuffering because He doesn't want anyone to perish.

In response to this great love and the sacrifice made for us, we are to love Him and the people He created. Just as God sees us through the blood of Christ as His children, we are to see others in light of the grace God gives us. We are to operate in a space of grace with our brothers and sisters, forgiving them quickly, searching for those who have gone astray and restoring them to the fold gently. When we are doing the work of restoration or forgiving others, we are to remember the sacrifice made to restore us and how God has forgiven us.

As much as God tells us to remember, He also calls us to forget. When we forgive someone, we are to forget the offense has taken place. It's as if they never trespassed or transgressed against us. When we truly forgive, we forget. We are also to forget those things behind us. What's behind you? Your accomplishments are behind you. How you did or didn't live for Christ last week is behind you. Sins you repented of are behind you. Days you've already lived are behind you. You cannot live in the past, whether you have a mansion or a prison behind you.

Paul says we are reaching and pressing for the mark of the high calling of God (Phil. 3:13-14). In order to reach, I need an empty hand. I have to let go of something to grab hold of something else. My focus needs to be on what I'm reaching for, not what I've released in order to reach.

The bible tells us repeatedly to remember the sacrifice God made for us. It doesn't tell us we need to remember every sin we've committed and flagellate ourselves over them after we have repented and confessed them. When we are helping others who are caught in a sin, we should remember the love and gentleness God delivered us with, and exhibit it to the one we are attempting to help. It is not so much the specific sin we are to consider but the nature of the deliverance.

In our faith journey, what we choose to forget is just as important as what we choose to remember. It determines whether we are stuck in the past or moving with a purpose towards the future God has for us. If our forgetting frees us from the past and allows us to pursue the will of God, it is good; if our forgetting entrenches us more firmly in our sin, it is bad.

We cannot become so wrapped up in what we used to do that we can't properly focus on what God is calling us to do now. Whether our past is littered with sin or sanctification, we cannot live life as if that past is the present. Forget what is behind. Remember how God loved you and saved you. It should be easy to remember because God is still loving you and still saving you right now.

God hasn't changed nor has He died. He is the same yesterday, today and forever. His intentions toward us are the same. Once we start to pursue Him, we need to continue to do so. No matter how long we've been pursuing Him, we need to keep pursuing Him until He catches us up into the heavens and takes us to the place He has prepared for us.

- **They go where they want despite redirection and warning.** The person I worked with would often attempt to leave the facilities. They were intent on going where they thought they were supposed to be going. This person had to be continually redirected. It was a task to get this person to understand they were where they were supposed to be. It was even more of an effort to convince them they knew the people who cared for them and they weren't being imprisoned or restricted but cared for and protected. It was hard to gently coax this person back into some semblance of reality. This person lashed out at us verbally and physically because they believed we were preventing them from keeping appointments or taking care of responsibilities they no longer had.

Sometimes we feel like this in our lives. We are confident we have places we need to go and responsibilities we need to meet. Yet people and circumstances keep redirecting and rerouting us. Nothing looks the way it would if we were on the right route, but we are afraid to admit we might be lost. Admitting we are lost means we made a wrong turn somewhere. It means we acted out of our will and followed our desires. It means maybe God didn't guide us, nor did He go with us.

Just because you don't recognize your surroundings or know where you are, however, doesn't mean you're lost. You could be exactly where God wants you to be. If God is taking us somewhere we haven't been before, chances are we will encounter places on the journey unfamiliar to us. We may experience doubt or uncertainty in the will of God when He moves us into new territories. What people suffering from spiritual Alzheimer's experience is different. When we plow ahead in certainty and end up outside of the will of God, we can end up in the valley confused about how we missed the mountain. It's disconcerting to think everything you think about your life is no longer true. Not only do your surroundings start to look unfamiliar, it may be difficult to recognize yourself!

If it is difficult to convince someone they aren't where they think they are, it can be neigh to impossible to persuade them they are not on the path or trajectory they should be on to get to where they want to go. One of the biggest obstacles to true communication, healing, and communion with Christ is our inability to perceive and admit fault. In our stubbornness, we refuse to turn from our ways and walk in The Way--that is, Christ. We think we can serve Him how we feel comfortable serving Him, give to Him what we feel comfortable giving Him of our time, money, energy, and effort, and take from Him whatever we think we need to do whatever it is we want to do. We forget God has commands and guidelines for how we are to interact with Him and with others. He tells us who we are to have fellowship with and who we are not to fellowship. He tells us how to worship Him and what type of worship He will not accept. He chooses to use us in whatever way He wants to for His glory. We don't get to dictate terms to God.

If we really are the church, the Kingdom of God, then we need to recognize the King of the kingdom. The King is the one who determines the edicts by which we live. He can call into His service anyone He wishes. No matter who He sends with the message, the message needs to be heeded. His message supersedes anything we had planned, anything we wanted to do, any place we intended to go.

- **They lash out when corrected.** The confusion and anger my client responded to me with are similar to the response of Christians who feel like their lives are not hitting the marks. They aren't where they feel they're supposed to be when they thought they would be there. This happens when reality breaks with the timeline or the vision we have in our heads of how things are supposed to go. It happens when we are in relationships with people and realize the relationship isn't going where we thought it was going. It happens when we reach a certain age without having accomplished a certain thing—marriage, children, careers, positions, homeownership, or being debt free or financially solvent. It happens when we or someone we love has to move or something else happens where we feel displaced. We become disoriented.

Oftentimes, we become angry about this disorientation. We can't understand why people can't get with the program or why our circumstances aren't lining up with our vision for this time in our lives. Why aren't we seeing what we are supposed to see if we are where we think we are? The reason we aren't seeing the markers of a specific location is because we aren't in that location. It can be difficult to process the anger and frustration associated with realizing we are off course. It's even more difficult to process the possible feelings of shame, embarrassment, or disgrace at not having lived up to our dreams and expectations. To avoid dealing with these feelings of inadequacy and abasement, we may seek refuge in denial.

When I cared for a person with Alzheimer's, one of their goals was to be oriented to time and place. Consequently, one of the things we had to do was ask the person several questions: What day is it? Where are you? Who am I? These questions were to gauge how lucid the person was at any given time.

What stands out to me the most is asking this person suffering with Alzheimer's where they are at any particular moment. To see the certainty melt away into confusion and frustration when they are told they are incorrect was difficult to see. It's scary to think someone can become lost in their own life. Every place they go becomes unfamiliar, even if they've been going there for years. When someone is mentally in another time or space, the markers of their everyday lives are gone. They are looking for landmarks and people they won't find.

The first step in the process of getting serious is to understand where you are and where you're heading. Take in your surroundings and the people in them. Based on what you read in God's word and know to be true, where do the landmarks around you indicate you are? What about the inhabitants of the land? Are the people you associate with the most and in the most intimate ways indicative of the place you're supposed to be? Do they seem to be heading in the direction you are intending to go? Is the path you're on clearly lit or is it shadowed and dark?

When someone has Alzheimer's, people can tell. The specific symptoms associated with the disease are easily identifiable by people who know the individual. We understand the individual's perception has become skewed by physiological changes in their body. We understand their mind is being ravaged and it is affecting what they see and how they see it.

When we suffer from spiritual Alzheimer's, we are not seeing the world around us clearly. It is a disease of the mind that affects our perception of reality. The very faculties we use to make sense of our world are malfunctioning.

Once the disease has a good grip, it's hard to slow its spread. It affects everything. If we have surrounded ourselves with spiritual people, these people will attempt to redirect us. They will keep reminding us of who we are, where we are, and where we're supposed to be going. This frustrates and angers the individual who is insistent on being right.

The danger in refusing correction is if we refuse to bend, we will suddenly be broken beyond repair (Pro. 29:1). It is up to us to be amenable to wise counsel and the word of God, to be sensitive to these things. Those pricks in our hearts need to be acted upon, not ignored and certainly not struck out against in anger.

A lot of the frustration Alzheimer's patients feel is because they believe that people are lying to them. They feel like people don't understand and don't know. Everyone has a problem but them. They know what they know.

God is very clear. He is saying to us "I haven't moved. I am here. If you aren't close to me, it means you are not where you're supposed to be." Maybe this means you aren't where you thought you were. Maybe it means you're exactly where you think you are, but it's not where you're supposed to be.

God isn't lying to us. He's not deceiving us or making things difficult for us. He isn't trying to trick us or ruin our lives. He is not the author of confusion (I Cor. 14:33).

Do you know where you are and are you going to accept what God is telling you about where you are? Because if you're not going to accept it, we don't need to discuss it.

Spiritual Alzheimer's, unlike the physical disease, is not irreversible. God can cure us. God sees you. God knows where you are. He knows where you've been. He knows where you're headed. Whether He put you there or you put yourself there, God knows exactly where you are.

Moreover, God is willing to work with where you are to get you where He wants you to be. The way back is through Christ. Christ said "I am the Way, the truth and the life (John 14:6)." If you want God to order your steps and be the driving force in your decisions and the guiding force in your life, then you have to allow God to be the Way and lead the Way back to peak spiritual health.

CHAPTER ELEVEN

Bitter, Broken, but Blessed

> Some people don't see it, but God's working in everything. ~Bro. Maurice Blackmon

Loss, especially losses we can't anticipate or adequately prepare for, can rob us of our faith. Grief can steal our belief in good things happening in our lives. If we aren't rooted in the word of God and if we aren't committed to having a relationship with the Lord, loss can cause us to question things. Grief can throw us off track and derail us, but if we have the right perspective, we can continue to grow while in a season of grief.

There are many different types of losses: the loss of a loved one; losing a relationship you've had for a long time; letting go of what you thought a relationship would be; being fired or laid off from a stable job you've worked for years; retiring and no longer having the structure or daily interactions with people you once did; or losing money in the stock market or real estate crashes. Anytime we lose something of value to us, we can be confronted with a sense of loss or grief.

How we respond to loss will determine whether the situation grows us or withers us. In the parable of the sower, we see tribulations can burn, wither or kill what the seed of the word is growing in our hearts. The circumstances of life and the cares of the world can choke out what God's word grows in us. We have to be rooted in ourselves to be able to use the tribulations we face like a plant uses the sun to create the food it needs to grow. We must view loss and grief with an understanding of what has taken place but also as an agent of growth.

This can be hard to do, since the nature of loss and grief seems negative. It seems final. No matter how much lead time we have, we are never prepared for it. Not only must we battle the circumstances, we must battle our feelings. Grief unleashes a flood of sadness and pain. On top of these feelings, we can also experience regret, guilt, anger, helplessness, inadequacy, abandonment, and fear.

How do we begin to wrap our minds around the reality of loss, let alone grow from the experience?

First, we have to recognize what loss is. Loss is a separation, a death. It's a failure to keep or continue to have something. It's when something is taken from you or destroyed. Loss puts a barrier between you and something or someone. This barrier either prevents you from experiencing something you're used to experiencing and/or ends any possibility of ever experiencing it. You will never get to celebrate Christmas with your loved one again. You'll never be able to reconcile with them. This sudden ending of possibility creates what we consider to be grief.

Grief is more than sadness. It's a mixture of sadness, pain, longing, and helplessness. It can often be mixed with regret. We tend to think of what we could have or should done differently. We wish we could take decisions back. We wish we could go back and do things we refused to do. What has happened has cut off all possibility of anything else. This separation and ending can be hard to comprehend and get over.

The bible speaks about death and loss in several different ways. Let's explore some of the responses to grief and death we find in God's word and use them to inform how we can move forward in grief in our lives.

Bitter & Empty (Ruth 1)

One example of someone grieving is Naomi. Naomi and her family left Bethlehem-Judah fleeing a famine. They found food, shelter and a place in the community in the land of Moab. Naomi's husband dies. Her sons marry Moabite women. After a while, Naomi's sons die as well. Naomi decides to return to her country, but she is emptier than when she left out. She is going back to her people without her husband and sons. At this point, she tells her daughters-in-law she is too old to have children and those children would take too long to grow up. She encourages them to go back to their people and their father's houses and find themselves new husbands. She pushes them away in her grief.

Even when she gets back to her community, around people who love her and are ready to embrace and take care of her in her loss, she still pushes others away. She tells the people not to call her Naomi but Mara, because the Lord has dealt so bitterly with her (v. 20). A root of bitterness has sprung up in her heart.

We can push people away when we are grieving. Not only can we push away those close to us who may also be sharing in our grief, sometimes we push away people who try to help—people in the community who come together to try and embrace us. We push everyone away to prevent anyone from getting close to us again. We want to prevent ourselves from ever experiencing this level of pain again.

The only problem is, this doesn't work. Pushing people away doesn't prevent us from experiencing loss. If we push people away, then we will lose something we *do* hold fast to, like money or security.

There is no way to avoid loss and pain. Moreover, we shouldn't seek to avoid them. Trials and tribulations work to create and develop character. Pain has a purpose.

Full of Fear (Gen. 38:6-11)

Another example of how we deal with grief is found in the story of Judah, his sons, and his daughter in law Tamar. Judah's first son Er married Tamar. He did evil in the sight of the Lord, and God smote him. In Jewish custom, when a man dies, his brother is supposed to marry his widow and have a child with her to carry on his brother's name (Deut. 25:5-6). According to the custom, Judah's next son, Onan, married Tamar. Onan does not want to have a child credited to his brother, so when he sleeps with her, he spills his seed on the ground so she can't get pregnant. God sees this as an evil thing and God kills Onan.

Now Judah has lost two sons at this point, but the law still hasn't been fulfilled and he still has another son. Instead of giving his last son to Tamar as he is supposed to, he tells her to remain a widow until his last son is grown. He makes her a promise he has no intention of keeping.

He's scared for his remaining son. What he wants to do is save his son from what killed his brothers. When we experience loss, we tend to gather up everything we haven't lost and hold on to it tightly. We may become anxious or frightened, afraid of losing someone or something else.

The problem is holding on tight doesn't prevent loss from occurring any more than pushing away and refusing to connect. It doesn't lessen the pain of loss. Instead, it only makes us angry we couldn't prevent the next loss despite our best efforts.

Hurting but Hopeful (2 Sam. 12:14-23)

If we know a loss is coming, we can begin grieving the loss before it happens. We experience dread and sadness knowing death is at the door. In the story of David and Bathsheba, God tells David because of his sin, his child is going to die. David begins to lay around in sackcloth and ashes, entreating the Lord to save his child. The whole time the child is sick, he won't eat. He's hoping his penance will change God's mind. He's in such a state his servants are afraid to tell him when the child dies. They don't know what he's going to do. But when they tell him, David arises, cleans himself up and gets a meal.

They marvel at this. David says

> while the child was yet alive, I fasted and wept: for I

said, Who can tell whether God will be gracious to me, that the child may live? ²³But now he is dead, wherefore should I fast? Can I bring him back again? I shall go to him, but he shall not return to me. II Sam 12:22-23

In this we see another response to grief: to seek and entreat the Lord, to really go after healing in an area, saving a relationship, healing of a person, or to keep a job when you sense a loss is coming. You are in prayer about it even though the loss seems inevitable. It's impossible with man, but you're hoping God will come through.

When the person dies, the relationship ends, or the job lays you off, there are two possible responses: we can let the disappointment break us, or we can have the response of David. David got up, literally cleaned himself up, and joined back in with the rest of the world. We can also go forward in faith. The person we love may be gone, but if they were in the household of faith they will be resurrected. The opportunity we lost out on isn't the last opportunity we will have to be in a successful relationship or have a good career. We have the choice to either believe God's going to provide and continue on, or to become bitter like Naomi.

What happens when we look for the Lord to prevent a loss and the loss happens anyway? What attitude should we have toward the loss? Are we able to view it as David viewed the loss of his son? Do we continue to look to the Lord in our grief?

When Grief Meets Grace (John 11:1-45)

Mary and Martha were looking for Jesus to come when their brother Lazarus was sick. They expected Jesus to come to His friend's side and heal Lazarus. Instead, Lazarus died before Jesus came.

Martha hears Jesus has come and runs out to meet Him. She tells Jesus she knows if He would have been there, Lazarus wouldn't have died. She also believes Jesus can still do something. She knows if Jesus asks God, God will do what He asks. She believes in the resurrection and knows her brother will rise at the last day. She confesses her belief in Jesus and His assertion He is the son of God.

Martha goes and tells her sister, Mary, of Jesus' arrival. Mary runs out to Him and falls down at his feet. She also says her brother would still be alive if Jesus had been there. They are weeping, sad, and a little confused. But they do the best thing a brokenhearted person can do: they stay near Jesus.

We see these sisters sharing their sadness with Jesus. They're upset and crying. But they have given the matter over to Jesus. They know Jesus allowed this. They don't know why. They don't know what He's going to do in response to Lazarus' death. But they believe in Him and they trust Him.

Jesus resurrects Lazarus. As Christians, we know those who die in the Lord will be resurrected at His coming and will live with Him in glory. We believe in the resurrection power. We receive hope from scriptures like this. We understand death is not the end.

One of the hardest things to deal with is when people die outside of the Lord. The resurrection of the saints is not something they are going to partake in. We can feel a lot of regret and guilt because of this. Maybe we didn't do enough to convince the person to get saved. Beyond the guilt of not getting them saved, we have to come to terms with the fact we probably won't see them again. If we're really living for God and they didn't, we will experience an eternal separation.

A strong sense of loss can breed the root of bitterness we see spring up in Naomi. She becomes bitter because she doesn't understand what the Lord is doing. The Lord was calling Naomi back to her people. She was out somewhere she wasn't supposed to be. God was calling her back to her people, and He was going to do something great through Ruth. In the midst of suffering and grief and anguish, we can't see all God is doing. We may never in this life see all of what God was doing in a situation. It requires a level of faith designed to stretch us to maintain our trust in God working all things together for our good.

Open Hands (Job 1:13-22)

Let's look at one last example of dealing with death in scripture to complete this picture. Job had ten children and they all died at the same time. He also lost all his livestock and livelihood the same day. Everything gone in a day. Before one person stops speaking, another comes with another bad report, and another, and another. It keeps getting piled on. His wife even loses faith. She tells him to curse God and die.

Everyone around him thinks he has done something to deserve this. We know he didn't do anything to deserve it. It seems unfair. But his response in faith is, "I have received good at the hand of the Lord; why not bad? God gave it to me and God can take it away." He has open hands about what most of us would find devastating.

Job isn't unaffected by his losses. We see him mourning and not being able to be comforted for some time (2:11-13). He mourns his children. But he understands God is in control. Even though he doesn't get it completely right—God didn't take those things away from him; the devil did—he is willing to accept God's will in his life, whatever it might be.

This is the appropriate response. We can try to make sense of loss or find the good in it. We can do whatever we want to do with it, but the most important thing is to trust God. We have to trust God has a reason or purpose for everything, and whatever the purpose, whether we ever know it or not, we trust God to get us through those situations.

But we're human. We do experience grief when we are confronted with loss. We wish things could be different.

Seeing the picture of Jesus—who weeps when He goes to Lazarus' grave, who has compassion for a widow who has just lost her only son, who is touched by a man who comes to Him requesting help for his sick daughter, and countless others recorded in scripture or lost in time—we see great compassion for people who are suffering. He knows what it's like to suffer grief and loss.

God knows what it's like to experience loss. God's Son died on the cross and He witnessed His Son's death. When Jesus died, the rocks broke open, the veil in the temple was rent, the earth was shaken, darkness covered the land, and the dead came out of their graves. All of these things show God's reaction to the death of Christ, who became sin for us. There's not a lack of understanding or compassion on God's part. God doesn't suffer from an inability to comprehend our loss. God understands that. Our objective or our mode of operation going through grief is to make sure we don't get stuck in grief and wither, that we don't pull away from God and wither and die in our grief.

"Walk Me"

When my great-aunt Pearlie Mae Carson was told she needed to get more exercise to combat health issues, I volunteered to walk with her. She would call me on the phone and say "Erica! Come walk me!" This expression was always funny to me. You walk a dog, not a person. But I didn't think much about it. I knew when she said it, it was time to put my trainers on and go.

During our walks, we walked all over. I don't think my great-aunt enjoyed walking. It was difficult for her at times, probably more difficult than I ever recognized. But one thing we both enjoyed was spending time together. Our conversations ate up the miles. We were going to the same place at the same pace, and we got through it together.

This is a powerful illustration of how we help others with grief, and how we deal with our grief. We're not always going to be able to motivate ourselves to keep going or get out of the grief by ourselves. We have to reach out to someone and say "walk with me through this." We may need someone else be an inspiration for us.

We won't want to do it. It's going to be difficult. But we'll have people willing to come alongside us and walk us through it.

Some of these people will have past experience and some won't. I didn't experience the health issues my great-aunt had. I didn't know how difficult it was for her to walk. But it didn't matter. Every day she called, I was ready to walk. If we needed to stop, then we stopped. If we needed to slow down, we slowed down, even though I wasn't tired. I was able to be the support she needed. I was in tune with where she was and knew when not to push so hard. But I also pushed when I needed to push. I could tell when she needed to push through, when she needed to overcome instead of sitting down in defeat.

On the other side of this, we are to mourn with those who mourn. The example of Job's friends' initial response is a good one. Sometimes you don't have words. You just sit with people. You be there. Be present. You allow them to lead conversations.

> I remember what God said in His word. He'll never leave us or forsake us. I think about the hymnal, No, Never Alone. I remember the first time I heard that after my husband's death, we were singing it in the congregation. I sat there and cried, right there in front of everybody... I would often cry in the middle of the congregation. Just sit there and weep. And I [would] make myself remember God's promises. Because He's not slack on His promises...Because He never goes anywhere. He's right there...~Sis. Zelda Jones

The bible specifically calls Christians to minister to widows and orphans, people who've experienced loss in specific ways. Sister Zelda Jones is a widow. Her husband died on a Saturday. She came to church the next day with her children. I admired the way she clung to her faith while dealing with the loss of her husband.

At the time, we had an atmosphere clouded with grief. Others had experienced the death of close family members within days of Sister Jones losing her husband. There was a lot of sadness and grief, but many of those people were still coming to worship. It was a testament not only to their faith but to the power of God. It encouraged, inspired and motivated me as someone who was supposed to be there for them, to see they were not wavering in their faith.

There is an initial rush for us to be there for people experiencing grief. This rush fades over time. Our regular life draws us back. People are still walking through grief, but we are no longer walking as closely beside them in it. It's not as personal for us. We don't have our hands on it all the time. It can be hard for us to remember who's going through what, or we figure it's been so long, they should be able to cope now. When we don't have this experience ourselves, it's easy to put time limits on feelings which simply don't exist.

Grief can be long term. There are no time limits. Sister Zelda Jones had a hard time. It was hard on her family. There were days she wasn't going to get out of bed, and sisters came to visit her or take her out. "Come on. Get up. Come with me. We're going to go do this." They continued to keep their hands on her and show her she wasn't alone.

Grief is an opportunity to grow in our faith—not only for the person who is grieving but for the people who attend to them. You learn so much from being there. You learn how God is faithful in grief. You see how He is close to the brokenhearted. It's the comfort and hope we get from scriptures, the hope of getting back what was lost and more. It's the assurance of seeing a loved one who died in Christ be resurrected. It's seeing God's love for us and knowing everything happens under his control and for our good. We get to see God's love in action through other Christians. We get to **be** love in action for other Christians. There aren't many more self-denying things we can do than helping someone who is grieving.

We can try to avoid grief all we want. It's going to catch up with us. We can do what we know to do to lessen grief, but what really helps people move forward in times of grief is to have people around them who love them and understand what they are going through. What helps is to have people who are willing to walk through this season with you.

So how do we apply this? How do we grow in a season of grief?

1. **We stay in God's presence through prayer.** When life brings us to our knees, we must decide we will go to God in prayer. Life is going to knock us down and things are going to happen. We need to be completely sold on the idea prayer changes things. It changes our hearts. There is a purpose for prayer. It comforts us. It guides us. It helps us to continue on.
2. **We stay wrapped in the word.** Through patience and comfort of the scriptures, we have hope (Rom. 15:4). Scripture helps us see other people of faith have gone through the same things and thrived. Scripture is a map to help us navigate through this foreign landscape of grief.
3. **We cannot sit down in grief and expect to grow.** We have to walk through it. We have to fight through it. That's how we grow. We cling to our faith in God's word—His promises and assurances. We count on Him to walk with us even if no one else does. We keep walking. We fight our way to a place of peace about what has happened.
4. **We have to pay attention to pain.** Pain is a signal. It provides information about what is happening. It is up to us to interpret this information, to filter it and decide how we will respond to it. There are instinctive responses and conditioned responses. Grief is a pain, and we react to it in the same ways we react to other painful stimuli. We have the examples of scripture and personal experience to determine how to respond, but the important thing is to respond. We can't shove it away and pretend it doesn't exist. The pain and sense of loss are there to teach us something.
5. **We must learn to trust in and run to God.** It helps us to grow when God does things we don't

understand and we have to trust Him. It helps us to grow when our faith is tested. Grief or loss of things we value will cause us to turn to what makes us feel safe and secure. We run from pain to things we feel won't hurt us the same way.

In grief, we run to what is familiar and comfortable. **Our response to grief shows where we really place our belief and trust.** Do we really believe the scripture? Is there something good in someone dying, in losing our house, job or relationship? How is God working any of this together for my good? Is it any of my business?

This is where real faith-work is done—when things don't go according to plan, when we don't get what we want. How can we bring glory to God in this?

6. **We must respond to grief as Christ did.** A good way to grow in these areas is to **see what Jesus' response to grief is**. Jesus' response to grief is empathy and compassion. We have to respond to others with empathy and compassion. We have to be able to go where they are and help them walk out. When we see others going through seasons of grief, when grief is all around us, do we have empathy? Does it move us? Can we understand what they are going through? Do we have compassion on them? Do we walk with them? Do we have faith in Jesus' ability to fix this situation and resurrect life from this death?

Like Martha, we sometimes tell Jesus "Lazarus has been dead for days. His body is starting to stink, and you're talking about resurrecting him." Do we trust God to resurrect something from the death and loss in our lives? Maybe by us losing all our money it's to the saving of our soul. Maybe it gives us a better appreciation of money so when we do have money again, we are better stewards of it.

7. **We have to look for what God is doing in every situation.** God works all things together for our good. He is close to the brokenhearted. He is a rewarder of those who diligently seek Him. Whatever we face in life, including grief, if we seek God, we will find Him.

CHAPTER TWELVE

A Woman in the Middle

⁴¹And Jesus answered and said unto her, Martha, Martha, thou art careful and troubled about many things: ⁴²But one thing is needful: and Mary hath chosen that good part, which shall not be taken away from her. Luke 10:41-42

Many of the women reading this are women in the middle—of both life experience and their Christian journey. You aren't who you used to be, yet you aren't who you ought to be. You are able to teach and able to be taught. Many are both older and younger, between their parents and their children.

Our lives are lived in the middle. The middle is the juicy part between the cradle and the grave where the good stuff can happen if we take advantage of it. It's where we dig in and decide a course for ourselves. It's where our lives are defined.

Being a woman in the middle means I've learned enough to realize I don't know anything. I'm living in the tension between being the teacher and the taught. I straddle the line between the "older woman" giving wisdom to my younger sisters and being the younger sister in need of an older woman's wisdom.

As I embark on different roles, I am stretched in opposing directions. It is in the midst of this push and pull I realize I need God more. I learn the ways in which He loves me most effectively when I am called upon to love others like He does in a new role. I'm finally hearing what God said and understanding it as well.

Now I'm being called on to be responsible for others. I realize the balance I need between filling my cup and pouring into someone else. I don't think of filling my cup as selfish but sustaining.

I knew I needed the Lord before, but now I *know*. I more fully appreciate how essential He is to life. The middle is where the perfect Christian in us goes to die so Christ can finally live in us.

Every Christian feels like Tennessee in the Civil War. There is a civil war going on in your life, with battles being fought on the inside of you as well as outside of you. The inside battle is your spiritual nature battling with your carnal nature. What the woman in the middle has to realize is, in order to have a thriving relationship with God in which her life produces fruit to His glory, she will have to win the wars in her heart and life.

Why would I say you're like Tennessee? Tennessee was a battleground state in the Civil War. Some parts of Tennessee fought with the Union and some parts fought with the Confederacy. Tennessee is second only to Virginia in the number of battles fought there during the Civil War because Tennessee was considered the gateway to the South. It contained waterways into the Deep South the Union wanted to control and the South wanted to defend. Tennessee is where the fighting took place.

We're where all the fighting happens. The devil is fighting with God over where your soul will spend eternity. This fight is made manifest in several areas of our lives: through disruption in our relationships, emotional upheaval, discouragement in comparison, striving, feeling unfulfilled, the struggle not to make an idol of people, money or things, struggling to do the right things we know to do, and struggling not to do the wrong things.

The devil is always looking to use a trial, tribulation, or transgression to snatch you back into His grasp. God is always working things together to bring about good for you. Both are using the same situations in your life to achieve their purposes. The question is, whose cause will advance in your life?

We are not neutral ground in this war. No, we have to choose a side. Jesus tells us clearly in Matt. 6:24 no man can serve two masters. Before he challenged the prophets of Baal, Elijah asked the people "how long halt ye between two opinions? If the Lord be God, follow him: but if Baal, then follow him (I Kings 18:21)." John is told in Revelations to write to the church of Laodicea: "I know your deeds, that you are neither cold nor hot. I wish you were either one or the other! So, because you are lukewarm—neither hot nor cold—I am about to spit you out of my mouth (Rev. 3:15-16 NIV)."

The bible doesn't give us a spiritual middle ground. Anyone who tries to live in the middle ground spiritually destroys themselves. A house divided against itself shall not stand (Matt. 12:25). A double minded man is unstable in all of his ways (James 1:8).

Further, God only gives us absolutes when it comes to serving and following Him. Anyone who chooses to be a friend of the world becomes an enemy of God (James 4:4). The light has no fellowship with darkness (II Cor. 6:14).

The spiritual middle ground is marked with indecision and frustration. Paul talks about the struggle in the middle ground: I find then a law, that, when I would do good, evil is present with me (Rom. 7:21). We struggle and fight the urge to give in to or flesh while we strive to do good things. It's an exhausting battle. Ultimately, Paul points us to Christ as the answer for deliverance from living in the spiritual middle.

Living by the law of the Spirit frees us from the law of the flesh. God called us from darkness and into His marvelous light (I Pet. 2:9). He delivered us from darkness (Col. 1:13).

We may be in the middle in the continuum of life, but God does not give us a spiritual middle ground, nor a set amount of time to choose where we stand. The end can come for us at any time and we have to be prepared for it. This is why it's so important for us to be serious about

Christ in whatever season we find ourselves. Woe to anyone who has not put on Christ and worked out her soul salvation when the books are opened in judgement!

Once you have chosen a side in this civil war, you have to stick to your decision. Anyone who puts His hand to the plow and looks back is unworthy. We must not look to the right or to the left, but straight ahead to the Father. As the song says, when we decide to follow Jesus, there is no turning back. We must press forward in faith.

You also have to train. You train by studying to show yourself approved (II Tim. 2:15). We know the word of God is sharper than a two edged sword (Heb. 4:12). We've talked about the importance of studying, the attitude we should have toward God's word, and how to study effectively.

The second part of training is to begin rightly applying the things you have studied. You must learn how to carry and use your weapon at the appropriate time. A fully loaded weapon is only as effective as the person who wields it. It does no good to have a fully loaded weapon you can't use. A loaded gun is an ineffective weapon if you don't know how to take the safety off, aim or shoot.

You also have to know which weapon to use in each battle you find yourself fighting. The word is a weapon we can use to defeat the devil, but we have to know which verse or passage of scripture to use when. Don't fight what the word tells you to flee, and vice versa. Rightly divide the word. Sharpen your senses by reason of use so you may have discernment and develop understanding.

You must learn how to identify allies and enemies. We wrestle not against flesh and blood, but against principalities, against powers, against the rulers of the darkness of this world, against spiritual wickedness in high places (Eph. 6:12). Even if a person seems to be doing something to you, they are not the enemy. They are not who you need to attack. This knowledge informs your battle plan and how you fight the battle.

If you mistake an ally or a civilian for an enemy, you lose sight of the real enemy. You are susceptible to attack because you're distracted. If you mistake an enemy for an ally, you run an even greater risk of being wounded in battle. We must be alert and diligent in this battle.

Avoid engaging in friendly fire. Friendly fire is when you attack others fighting with you while attempting to attack the enemy. This happens through misidentification, error, or inaccuracy. You don't want to be a person who shoots a sister down with friendly fire.

How do we do this? With gossip, slander, backbiting, and pessimism. We commit murder with our mouths. We assassinate each other's character. We wound with our words. We kill one another spiritually with a smile on our face because we have misidentified each other. We think we have scored a victory for our side when we've weakened the body.

If you're going to be a soldier, you have to be aware of these things. You have to be sure you're fighting the real enemy, and you know how to use the weapons you've been given. You have to know which weapons to deploy and the right time to deploy them.

Fighting with the word is a good skill to have, but it doesn't always help you to move from the middle. You can spend all of your time defending against the attacks of the devil and never move forward. If you are going to move forward in life, you have to advance. Advancement is the only sure way to victory.

How do you move from the middle ground and the battlefield mentality of life? The best strategy is to go on the offense. Here are my battle tested tools for moving forward even while fighting the enemy:

- **Prioritize**. In the story of Mary and Martha, Mary is upset because she is working while her sister is sitting at the feet of Jesus. When she asked Jesus to tell her sister to help her, He instead insists Mary has chosen the good part and it will not be taken from her. In our lives, we have to learn to prioritize the things necessary for our growth and advancement, the things which advance the cause of Christ, over our comfort or our fear. We have to decide for ourselves to embrace sitting at Jesus' feet as the good part and refuse to let anyone or anything take it away from us. If you have to get up earlier, stay up later, forego lunch with friends or coworkers, or change what you listen to while you work out, make the extra effort to spend time with Christ, in prayer and in the word. Move away from what you think about God, Jesus, and the Holy Spirit, and start to add to the things you *know*.

- **Set aside every sin and weight so you can run (Heb. 12:1).** It is easy to identify sin when you are reading God's word, but how do you identify a weight? A weight isn't the same thing as a sin. A weight is anything which hinders you or keeps you from doing what you should do. Paul tells the Galatians, you were running well; who hindered you that you should not obey the truth (Gal. 5:7)? People, pursuits, and possessions, while not sinful, can be a weight if they hinder us from following Jesus wholeheartedly. We must lay aside anything causing us to stumble or stagger under its weight.
- **Walk/run.** An object in motion tends to stay in motion. We are to walk in the light as God is in the light. Each step forward takes us further from the indecision and stagnation of the middle ground. We can't stand in the way of sinners or sit in the seat of the scornful (Psalm 1:1). We can't afford to get mired in inactivity.
- **Abide in Christ.** Anyone who abides in Christ will grow (John 15:5). Growth means you aren't stagnant. In Christ you can do all things; apart from Him you can do nothing. Lean into the Lord's presence and seek it every day.
- **Capture or Be Captured.** We are exhorted

to take captive every contrary thought to make it obedient to Christ (II Cor. 10:5). We are told we were made free by Christ and not to make ourselves the slaves of men (I Cor. 7:23). Christ set us free. We are free indeed. But many of us stay in the middle ground because we don't want to offend people by choosing a side. We are more concerned about what people think of us, what everyone else is doing, or the impact of our profession of faith on our standing than we are about what God would have us to do! No one can win the fight for their soul if they aren't committed to capturing rogue thoughts. No one can win the fight who isn't intentional about being free from the shackles people would place on them if they were dependent on people's opinions and approval for every move they make.

It's time to shift our focus, ladies. We're all busy with our everyday lives and feel as if we can't add one more thing to our plates. But if we are going to be serious about growing an intimate relationship with Christ, we have to prioritize our relationship with Him. We have to be interested in the things which interest Him. And Christ is interested in the lost. He's interested in our sisters. He's interested in the good part. We need to be as well.

CHAPTER THIRTEEN

The Ministry of "She"

Too often, everything we do for others starts with us and not with Jesus or the gospel. The point of the ministry of me was to recognize who God is, who He created you to be and how we should treat others in the light of those two things, the ministry of "she" explores how we must position our hearts when it comes to serving others. What is our motivation for sharing the gospel and serving others? How do the disciplines we practice in secret to develop our relationship with God overflow into how we minister to others? How do we consider ourselves when restoring those who have been overtaken in sin?

Many people believe ministry is only an outward process. While it is true ministry is the labor we do to benefit others, ministry is the fruit of an inward process. Just as how we view God changes how we view ourselves, and vice versa, how we practice the "secret" disciplines and what motivates us to serve others changes how we serve them.

There are many ways to serve others. The talents, testimonies, and temperament you have all factor into how you serve, but they are not the basis for why you serve. Many Christians get these things mixed up.

We think because we are good at a particular thing, we should be out front and center anytime it is needed:

- I'm a great singer, so anytime a song leader is needed, I should be chosen.

- I'm a great speaker so I should be able to preach.
- I've had five kids, so anytime anyone has an event talking about child rearing, I need to be the first one they call.
- I've gone through a particular experience, so someone needs to give me a microphone to talk to other women about it.

We think our disposition determines how God will ask us to serve:

- I don't have any patience for children, so I know the Lord doesn't want me to teach Sunday school or serve in the nursery.
- I love young people, so I know the Lord called me to lead the youth ministry.
- I love organizing, so God must want me to plan the Ladies' Day.

None of this is how it really works. God has qualifications beyond talent, testimonies, and temperament for the positions we serve in, "official" or not. God expects us to use our particular gifting to accomplish His will, but He has already given us a "why" independent of our gifts.

What do I mean by this?

We are to do all things to the glory of God. God wants us to make disciples of Christ. We are called to assist in the saving of souls (Matt. 28:19-20), to train children up in the nurture and admonition of the Lord (Eph. 6:4), respect the older when we are younger (I Pet. 5:5), teach the younger when we are older (Titus 2:3-5), submit to our husbands (Eph. 5:22), obey the ordinances of the law (Rom. 13:1-14), care for orphans and widows (James 1:27), and do good to all but especially those of the household of faith (Gal 6:10). We are to be a city on a hill (Matt. 5:14), a light on a lampstand (Matt 5:15), and the salt of the earth (Matt. 5:13). We are to run with patience the race set before us (Heb. 12:1)—all to the glory of God. All to know Christ and make Christ known.

I don't serve others because I'm uniquely positioned by my natural abilities, education, and experiences to do the particular thing I'm doing: I allow God to use all the abilities and experiences He put into my life in whatever way will bring Him glory.

We aren't all given the same amount of talent, and we aren't all talented in the same areas. But God expects all of us to use the gifts He gave us. He expects a return on His investment. Just as in the parable of the Unfaithful Servant, He expects us to put what He gave us to use.

But I am not expected to produce the same amount of fruit as anyone else. Just as Jesus says, some produce a hundredfold, some sixty and some thirty (Matt 13:8, 23). We can't look to others in ministry and see how many people they have led to baptism, fed, clothed, prayed for, studied with, or taken in and judge what we are contributing to the body of Christ by their output. We don't even know if they are doing all this and will still be told by Jesus He never knew them (Matt. 7:21-23) or if they will be a castaway (1 Cor. 9:27).

People do things in the name of Jesus for reasons other than to bring Him glory, and Jesus tells them firmly He never knew them. Sisters, our heart in service matters. We are to give as we've purposed in our heart, cheerfully (II Cor. 9:7). When we ask for things from God, it can't be only to our benefit (James 4:3).

If Christ is really our example, we have to have a heart for people. We must be compassionate and seeking to save the lost. Jesus said He didn't come to condemn the world but to save it (John 3:17, 9:56).

Can you imagine how much different Jesus' ministry would have been if He had come to condemn us instead of save us? He would have looked for any little reason to disqualify us from being heirs of God instead of looking for ways to extend mercy and grace. But Jesus was mindful of the mission God sent Him on. Everything He did on earth proved He came to save the world and not condemn it. We have to be mission-minded as well if we are going to serve others well.

Our mission is to seek and save the lost. We are to use all the things God gave us to accomplish this goal. We are not here for others to marvel at how talented we are or to feed our need for recognition of who we are. We are here to be arrows pointing the way to Jesus. We are more than willing to fit in the body wherever God has placed us and function however He wants us to because it isn't about us at all.

So what if I have more degrees, more public speaking experience, and can structure a sermon better than my minister? God gave strict criteria for ministers to be measured against, criteria I don't meet. God placed who He wanted in the minister's seat. It doesn't matter if I am a better planner than the sister selected to be over the ladies' day, or if the children like me better than the Sunday school teacher for their class. Has God called me to take the position? Do I meet all the qualifications? Who or what am I trying to satisfy?

Beyond the motivation of saving souls and giving glory to God, we have to love people.

Before we could talk about discipleship, mentoring, or female relationships in light of growing in Christ, we needed to position ourselves appropriately in this narrative by understanding who God is, who/what He created us to be, and the real passion behind our purpose. We needed to till the soil of our hearts and cultivate this ground in order to plant God's word on service to others in good ground.

We must examine ourselves and our motivations before we stand in front of the judgment seat of Christ. We must see to our condition. We have to know what dysfunctions or deficiencies we bring to the table in this area so we can ask God to fix them. We can't grow if we don't.

The other side of the coin is what we are supposed to do toward others. It's not just about us, our selfish ambition, or furthering ourselves. It's not making sure we make it to Heaven without thought to anyone else. We are called to teach others. We are called to baptize them and teach them again. We are called to visit widows and orphans and take care of their needs. We are to encourage, exhort, and restore one another. If someone is overtaken in a fault, the spiritual are to restore them (Gal. 6:1). We are supposed to love one another. People seeing how we love one another is supposed to point them to Christ. This is how they know we are His, if we have love one for another (John 13:35).

How do we show other people Christ? I'm not talking about how we say it. I don't mean saying to someone "I'm a Christian" or verbally giving God glory. Are we showing people we are Christians by them seeing our good works, by them seeing what we do toward one another?

The bible says we are to practice some disciplines in secret and God will reward us openly (Matt 5:2, 6). Prayer is one of these disciplines. If you pray before men, using big words and vain repetitions to showboat and puff yourself up, you have your reward when people tell you how beautiful and uplifting your prayer was (Matt. 5:5). Every time someone tells you your prayer was moving or beautiful isn't an indication you were showboating or you had the wrong motivation. But if our motivation is incorrect, we can lead others to salvation and ourselves be castaways (I Cor. 9:27). Even if we make an outward show of glorifying God, God will judge our hearts.

We must be careful not to let what we do for others serve to satisfy our selfish ambition instead of serving the individual. We must examine whether or not we are doing things to make ourselves look or feel good or to bring recognition to ourselves. Getting a good feeling from doing something is not the purpose of doing it. Feeling good about donating your time, your money, or your effort isn't bad, but it's not the purpose behind these actions. You don't do it to feel good; you do it to honor God.

Ministering to others to please God requires me to get outside of myself and my comfort zone. It requires talking to people I wouldn't associate with if it were up to me, but who I am called on to share the gospel with as Christ did. I can't hide the gospel from people who don't look a certain way or haven't acquired a certain amount of possessions. I may be called to show God's love and share the gospel with people who have been on drugs, who are homeless, dirty, castoffs of society. Prostitutes need the gospel the same as virgins do. People who have mental illness and are often overlooked need to be shown the love of Christ.

If I am going to really live out my faith, I have to do more than read the Bible for myself; I have to share it. I have to do more than pray for myself; I have to go before the Lord for my sisters and brothers in Christ. I have to go beyond handing out a meal so I can feel good about myself. I have to stop posting my good deeds to social media for validation and pats on the back. I have to stop doing everything in a desperate attempt to point people to my righteousness and instead make sure everything points to Christ and our Father in Heaven.

We can't say we are serious about our walk with Christ and doing the Lord's work if we aren't serious about God getting the glory for what we're doing for others. Making sure I'm together isn't the end of my mission. I should have a proper perspective on who I am and my relationship with Christ and others. I should know everyone who has been baptized into Christ has put on Christ and we are all equal in Him.

If I really believe we are all in the family of God, I should have a brother/sister relationship with others in Christ. I should be able to share Christ with anyone who wants to learn about Him, whether they are socially acceptable or not. Whether they have struggles people would label worse than others or not. God is not a respecter of persons and I shouldn't be either.

Having ourselves in the proper perspective and being aware of areas in which we need to minister to ourselves is important. Studying God's word, praying, fasting, almsgiving, tithing, and cultivating fruit of the spirit are all important. We must nourish our spiritual being as much as we do our physical. But we must be vigilant in guarding against turning self-care into self-worship, idolizing or puffing ourselves up, and closing ourselves off.

When we are doing for others as the Bible commands,

we are not doing it to fulfill selfish ambitions, to assuage guilt or as penance. We aren't making the work about us but we are focused on being the arrow pointing to Christ. We are focused on being obedient to Him and showing Him faithful to His promises. We are reflecting His glorious light so it shines in the darkness of a lost world and lights the way for the lost to be found. We are seeking to be the light by which others see the Lord for who He is and give Him the glory and honor due Him.

CHANGING SEASONS

Spring is a fickle season characterized by swift changes. There are times when you have planted and something starts to grow. Then the weather changes and kills off the tender shoots and buds you began to see.

The uncertainty of the season can cause us to doubt. When you start to see a little progress and then the endeavor isn't supported or the work fizzles out and dies, it can be hard to trust you can bring forth fruit the next time.

The appearance of loss may be a harbinger of the fruit to come. Orange groves and cherry trees have beautiful flowers in the springtime. These die in a matter of a week or two. This occurs naturally to make room for the fruit they will produce. The blossoms look good, but they aren't supposed to have longevity or consistency.

If we aren't aware of this, the appearance of the situation can cause us to be doubtful. We have to know what we're supposed to produce. Is it supposed to look like this? Am I supposed to produce a flower or a fruit?

When those flowers die, it's a natural illustration of someone in doubt. This thing you've worked for has flowered. The seed you planted has budded and flowered. It's blossomed and appears to be growing. But the blossom falls off quickly and you have no guarantee anything else is going to grow there. You don't know something of more substance, something with the capability to sustain life, will replace the beautiful but useless blooms. You can sustain life off of oranges, cherries and apples, but you can't from those flowers.

It's in these seasons of life we have to ensure we are acting in faith and not operating in doubt. Doubt is a virus. It finds an opening and spreads throughout our lives, multiplying itself. If left unchecked, doubt will paralyze us, killing our faith and severing our relationship with Christ.

Over and over again in scripture, God speaks against doubt. Jesus said those who doubted were not His sheep because they didn't know His voice (John 10:24-27). He told the disciples if they believed and did not doubt, they could move mountains (Matt. 17:20). James said a man who wavers, or doubts, should not expect anything of God (Jas. 1:6-7). We may think having doubts is normal, but doubt cannot coexist with faith. Just as perfect love casts out fear (I John 4:18), true belief casts out doubt.

Doubting causes us to forget all the ways in which God has kept His promises. When the children of Israel refused to take the land of Canaan, they had every reason to believe God would give them the land. God had shown them every god of Egypt was false. He had crushed their enemies. He fed them in a land with few natural resources. He kept them from predators. Yet they still didn't trust Him at His word. They were right next to the Promised Land. The spies confirmed what the Lord told them about the land being plenteous. But they allowed their perspective of the inhabitants of the land to keep them from claiming what God promised them. Even when two of the spies insisted they could take the land with God on their side, the people refused to move forward. Instead, they expressed their doubt and fear by accusing God of bringing them into the land to die.

Have you ever been standing on the cusp of walking into your Promised Land? Have you ever felt like you were at the tipping point in a life situation where you knew if you pressed forward in unmitigated faith, you could grab God's very best for yourself? Perhaps you feel that way now. Maybe you are graduating school with a job offer in another state or been offered a higher paying job at another company. Maybe you realize certain relationships in your life need to be severed and you're finally ready to cut ties.

Maybe you've been unemployed for a long time and just got a call back for a second interview. Maybe you just finished the first draft of a book or wrote the last note to a song. Maybe your side hustle has turned into a legitimate entrepreneurial pursuit and you feel like it's time to quit your day job and pursue your passion fulltime.

Whatever notable transition you are on the cusp of making, I urge you to go forward with God. If God is with you, trust Him to honor His promises. Stop comparing yourself to the competition. It didn't matter how big the inhabitants of Canaan were, how strong or how mighty; God would have won the fight for them if they had said to themselves "God has shown Himself faithful thus far. Even though we wouldn't be able to do it alone, we can do all things with God." Instead, they chose to believe their perception of themselves.

We've already discussed how the way we see ourselves determines how we see God, and vice versa. Well, the spies told the children of Israel they were like grasshoppers before the people in Canaan. They had the choice of trusting and believing God for victory or letting their own deficiencies outweigh God's power.

This is what we sometimes do when faced with challenges. It's like we forget God is in the equation. Not only in the equation, but the deciding factor. We have given ourselves the credit for where we have gotten. We default to weighing our abilities against the inherent challenges of moving forward. Many of us, while looking at Canaan and knowing what treasures it holds, stand outside of it and question why God has brought us here knowing we are no match for the challenges to taking ownership of the land. Many of us don't fail to conquer Canaan; we refuse to attempt to conquer Canaan when God has told us Canaan is ours.

Despite all God had done for them and shown them, the children of Israel couldn't conquer doubt. They looked at themselves and their abilities and not at God. They didn't take into account God's track record for keeping His promises. Why couldn't they trust Him? Because the children of Israel had been oppressed for so long, surviving attempted genocide, and having their spirits crushed by backbreaking labor and hundreds of years of what they saw as unanswered prayers, they had a difficult time trusting. Even though they left Egypt, they were still shackled by many of the ideologies of the land because it was familiar to them. Things had been the same for generations upon generations, and though things were bad, they were familiar.

Many of us know what we have isn't what we want. We know what is waiting for us promises to be better. But we don't know for sure. The challenge of faith is we are asked to move before we see the entire path. If we could see it completely, it wouldn't require faith.

We don't know how we'll handle all of the challenges over there. What if I don't like it or it doesn't live up to my expectations? What if I'm making the wrong decision? What if it wasn't really God telling me to leave my job or my relationship? What if I fail?

I know this man isn't the best for me, but I don't know if I'll meet a better man, and at least now I have a man. I hate my job but at least I can pay some of my bills. If I start a business and it fails, I won't be able to do even that much. I want to take this new job opportunity, but I don't know anyone in the state. I don't have a support system. My family and friends don't see me often and are never available when I need them now, and in fact aren't that supportive of a support system, but I don't want to be by myself.

Doubt causes us to question God. It can make us bitter. It can convince us God led us from our unsatisfying but tolerable existence into the wilderness to die. It makes us forget our vow to follow Jesus and the miraculous things He's done in our lives. It brings to our remembrance all the times we lost what we had without reminding us of the better we gained. Doubt keeps us from growing.

I told you being serious is not staying small because you're afraid of expanding into the new space God is trying to take you. I also told you it wasn't being afraid of how big you can be in Christ. But these fears are real. In order to grow, we need to learn how to fight fear.

Creating fear is a process which occurs in our subconscious. We experience a stimulus our brain must process and react to. Information is sent along two pathways in the brain simultaneously for processing, the low road and the high road. The low road doesn't take chances. It assumes the most dangerous source and seeks to protect us from harm. The high road is a slower road, but it collects more accurate information to help us determine how we should respond to a stimulus.

If you hear a strange noise outside, the low road initiates your fight or flight response while the high road begins processing information from your senses to provide meaning and context. The hippocampus, the part of the brain responsible for providing context, attempts to determine if it has seen this stimulus before and what the cause was the previous times it encountered the stimulus. If the hippocampus determines there is no danger, it sends a signal to the amygdala, the conductor of the low road, and the amygdala tells the hypothalamus to shut down the fight or flight response. The reason we feel terror and fear before we know what's really happening is because the information travels faster on the low road than the high road.

If we are going to fight spiritual doubt and fear, we have to train ourselves to ask, like the hippocampus, have I seen this before? Have I face a similar situation? What happened when I faced this before?

Remembering how God brought us through similar situations can help us to overcome doubt and fear. Meditating on what God has done for us helps us to increase our faith in His ability to bring us through the present trial.

As I stated before, true belief casts out doubt. But how do you cultivate faith? How much faith do I need? What characteristics should I be developing? Are there different levels of faith, and if so, how do I know where I am or how can I move from one to another?

Fig Tree Faith (Matt. 21:18-22, Mk. 11:12-14, 20-24)

Let's talk about fig tree faith. When Jesus was traveling with His disciples, He grew hungry. He spotted a fig tree with leaves on it. It looked good for food. When He came to it, He found it was nothing but leaves. No fruit was on the tree. Jesus curses the tree and it withers away quickly. Jesus uses this opportunity to teach His disciples about faith able to move mountains. He says if they believe and don't doubt, they will be able to tell a mountain to move and be cast into the sea and it will happen. He further says all things, whatsoever we ask in prayer and believe, we shall receive.

This is very similar to what Jesus said in Matt 7:7 in His sermon on the mount. At that time, He said ask and you shall receive. Now He is telling them to ask with faith.

Faith is the active ingredient in our prayers. It activates the power of them. But we have to ask with nothing wavering, or no doubting. James says in James 1:6-7 to ask in faith with nothing wavering. The man who wavers is like a wave of the sea being driven and tossed by the wind. It doesn't choose its destination or how fast it gets to it. It has no control. It is helpless. James says a man like this shouldn't think He will receive anything of the Lord.

All of this begs the question: Have you moved any mountains lately? Have you tried to? Is there a mountain standing in your way? How do you approach the mountains in your life? Do you try to walk around them? Do you try to climb them? Do you turn and go back? Or do you tell the mountain to get out of your way?

Whenever I would read this passage, I would think of a physical mountain and my mind would bogle. I would look like a crazy person going to a physical mountain, telling it to move and expecting it to happen. Mountains aren't going anywhere. They have to be accommodated and worked around. They have to be accounted for. My literal interpretation missed the spiritual implications.

A physical mountain is a mass of rocks and earth that,

over time, has become a gargantuan thing. It appears at first to be insurmountable. The closer to the top you go, the more treacherous the weather and the thinner the air becomes. Most people respect the inherent danger of tackling mountains. Many avoid it from fear. Others will attempt to climb it looking for an adrenaline rush. Many who attempt to climb a mountain turn back part way up, while others will perish in their attempt to conquer it.

Do you have things like this in your life? Things much bigger than you? Maybe you try to avoid them, but they are separating you from where you really want to go. You try to go around them, but you realize there's no way to get where you're going without going through this obstacle somehow. Maybe you start to climb but it becomes too much: the air becomes too thin, the journey is too strenuous, you run out of supplies—and you have to turn back. Maybe you attack mountain climbing with relish only to succumb to the elements, buried in an avalanche or falling off.

You know what mountain stands between you and the things you want, the things you feel called to do, the people you should be helping, or the "more" God has for you. It's not a "little" sin or a slight financial disadvantage: it's a towering thing blocking out everything else.

You've struggled with this thing every way you know how. Fought it with everything you have. Avoided it for as long as you could. Made promises, goals and resolutions you would get to the other side of it year after year and you still haven't managed to conquer it. We can call it what we want, but there's this towering, frightening thing set before us and if we are to have all the things God promised us— abundant life, peace, joy, fellowship with Him—we are going to have to deal with it.

Jesus says don't bother trying to climb it or go around it; just tell it to be removed and cast itself into the sea. This isn't avoidance; it's trusting God to do the heavy lifting. It's allowing Him to move the things we cannot without the limitations we tend to place on what God can do.

Mustard Seed Faith (Matt. 17:14-21; Lk. 17:3-6)

Mustard seed faith is different than mountain faith. When the Bible speaks of having faith the size of a mustard seed in Matthew 17, it is after the disciples of Jesus have tried to cast a demon out of a boy. Jesus casts the demon out and His disciples ask why they weren't able to do it. Jesus tells them it is because of their unbelief. If they had faith the size of a mustard seed, nothing would be impossible to them.

This is an encouragement after a defeat. They came up against something they couldn't cure and they took it to Jesus. He tells them some things are only accomplished through fasting and prayer. This is consistent with the fig tree example in which He says whatever they ask for in prayer without doubting, they will receive.

The other example of mustard seed faith is when Jesus tells the disciples they must forgive their brothers each time they trespass against them and repent. The disciples ask Jesus to increase their faith. Jesus again mentions faith the size of a mustard seed.

When they think they need more faith, when they meet opposition and fail, Jesus encourages them to have a little faith. This little seed of faith is going to grow and flower and produce fruit if you cultivate it. How do you cultivate it? Start using it.

Walking on Water Faith (Matt. 14:22-31)

Is this next level faith or what? The disciples see Jesus walking on water toward their boat. He isn't walking on the water on a smooth sea either; the wind is contrary and waves are tossing the ship. Peter asks Jesus to let him walk on the water to meet Him. When Jesus tells Peter to come, Peter steps out of the boat and he too walks on water. It is only when Peter notices the strong winds he begins to sink. Peter calls out to Jesus to save him, and Jesus does. But Jesus asks Peter why he doubted.

Jesus acknowledges the little faith Peter had. After all, Peter is the only one who got out of the boat to begin the journey to Jesus on the water even after Jesus identified Himself. Peter had enough faith to begin walking. But he didn't have enough faith not to be afraid. His fear caused him to doubt according to Jesus' words. He has a little faith, but he still has doubt and fear.

Jesus speaks to those of little faith several times in scripture explicitly to warn against anxiety, the teachings of the Pharisees, fear, and doubt. He does one of two things in these moments: either He reminds them of God's provision in nature or toward them in the past, or He gently rebukes them for allowing fear and doubt to shake their faith.

These are encouragements not to have faith, but to get rid of doubt. It shows us how to deal with doubt.

We all know there are many people who started this faith journey with us who are no longer walking with us. We know from our own experiences we can be operating in faith to do things far beyond what we imagined one moment and be sinking the next.

The encouragement we find in how Jesus dealt with crises of faith in His disciples can change our lives if we let it. Peter knew enough to call out to Jesus and let Jesus save him when he began to sink. The disciples asked Jesus to increase their faith and He encourages them by showing them all they needed was a little faith. It was only when they tried to reason together they were more strongly reprimanded.

We have to know who to ask for clarity when we are having a crisis of faith. We have to know who has all the answers. Jesus has told us whatever we ask for in faith without doubting we shall receive. This asking is of the Lord through prayer, not people. We don't need to reason with one another, our circumstances, our budget or anything else. Asking in faith, in true faith, trumps logic, shortcomings, projected outcomes, past experience, wise counsel, and anything else we can come up with.

Having faith breeds faith. We can look back and remember when God was faithful to His promise He would reward our faith.

How do you get more faith? The Bible says faith comes by hearing. What do you hear? The word of God. If you want more faith, you have to be hearing God's word. Reading and studying the Bible is important—no, integral—to your faith. If you haven't stepped out on faith and seen God reward you and work with this faith in your life, you can read about it over and over in the scriptures.

CHAPTER FOURTEEN

Discipleship, Mentorship, & Female Relationships

The Passion of the Christ came out my freshman year at Purdue University. On February 25, 2004, Campus Crusade for Christ (now known as Cru) gave free tickets and a ride to the theater to anyone who wanted to see the movie. There was a big push to get people to see and understand what Christ did for them on the cross.

Events like this can be a good tool for evangelism. There were a lot of people in the dorms who were not familiar with the crucifixion. There were international students who didn't grow up in a country where Christianity was a major religion. Some of them didn't have any exposure to Christ. Others had heard about the crucifixion, but couldn't picture what a crucifixion would look like.

Hundreds of people, perhaps a thousand, went to see The Passion of the Christ through this initiative. Many were emotionally pulled by what they saw. This is expected because of the emotional nature of the subject matter. The movie focuses almost exclusively on the beatings, whippings, and humiliation Jesus suffered from the time He was betrayed by Judas until he died.

I encountered a girl in the bathroom after the showing I attended who tearfully asked me why they killed Jesus this way. Until that moment, I didn't fully appreciate there were people who had never heard the story Jesus, His life and His crucifixion. It was looking into her tear filled eyes I became aware of the need to tell others the significance of

Jesus' death. If I didn't tell her, she wouldn't know it was to give her the opportunity to spend eternity with God.

Standing in a movie theater bathroom on a random Friday night as a college freshman was my first opportunity to share the gospel. This wasn't how I imagined this moment to go. I imagined I would be in a church with my bible on my lap and at least one experienced evangelist in the room to step in should I mess it up. Or maybe I would feel a charge like lightning go through me and God would speak directly out of my mouth. Instead, after a quick prayer, I answered the question she asked as simply and truthfully as I could.

This wasn't the last time I ended up having to share the gospel with no preparation while in college, but this bathroom encounter stands out in my mind as an example of everyday discipleship. The movie The Passion of the Christ provided many believers with a teachable moment where they could sit down with someone and tell them the rest of the story. It was an opportunity to help people understand who Jesus was, what He did, and how the truth of His life, death, and resurrection could transform their lives.

I don't know if the members of Campus Crusade for Christ were given any preparation prior to the screenings on how to follow up with the people who came. I believe they handed out pamphlets of some sort talking about Jesus, but I don't know if anyone would have sat down with the woman I spoke to in the bathroom to share the gospel with her. I certainly wasn't prepared for it. But I should have been.

You can't be serious about being a Christian if you're not serious about discipleship. Anyone who is serious about biblical discipleship is serious about the two fold mission of adhering to the teachings of our savior Jesus Christ and spreading the gospel to the creation of more disciples, or followers, of Jesus.

The definition of a disciple is "a convinced adherent of a school or individual." It is someone who both accepts and assists in spreading the doctrine of another. If we are doing discipleship right, we are adhering to the Gospel, accepting and convinced of its truth. We are also assisting in the spreading of Christ's doctrine.

We can't adhere to the teachings of Christ if we don't know what they are. We can't spread what we don't know effectively. We must be students of the word, but we need to do more than study the word; we need to share it.

No matter how long we've been Christians, there are things we are still learning or working on. God is still revealing more to us just like Christ continued to teach the disciples up until His death. After His death, Jesus continued to teach His disciples about the kingdom of God until His ascension. Paul says not as if he's apprehended, or learned all he can learn (Phil. 3:12). There's always going to be more we can learn.

At the same time, we have to discern when we have reached the maturity tipping point where we need to begin teaching others. You don't have to teach Sunday school or speak at conferences or ladies' days to teach. You can teach through conducting or participating in bible studies, through mentoring, or even through example. I want to encourage all women to do what the original disciples did—teach people about Christ, lead non-believers to baptism and continue to teach the new convert more about God.

The approach many of us take to spreading the gospel is to invite people to church and allow the minister to do the rest. Some are willing to tell people they need to "come to church" or they need God. But the thing is, *we*, the members, are the church, not the building. Getting them to the place where we meet for organized worship isn't as important as introducing them to the one true church, the community of the called out and set apart. It's not as important as introducing them to the gospel message.

No matter how good the singing is, how well someone prays publically, or how exciting and thought provoking your minister may be, the important thing for someone to come away with is a changed life from contact with God through obedience to His word. If all people get out of our service is a good time, entertainment, or assurance of blessings they aren't even qualified by the blood of Christ to be partakers in, then we are failing as a body of believers. Bringing someone to church for this is as effective as taking them to see a movie or play. They may ooh and ah in the moment. Their feelings of enchantment and awe may linger with them for a long time. But they won't return to everyday life forever changed. They won't be obedient to the saving of their soul.

There's nothing wrong with inviting someone to Sunday service, or any service, but it is our responsibility to make sure the person we bring hears the gospel and has an opportunity to respond. We haven't done our part by bringing them to a religious gathering.

If we don't feel capable of leading a bible study, we can lead people to someone who is capable. We can sit alongside them with our bible open and our hearts in prayer for them to accept the offer of eternal life being extended to them. We can contribute as we are led by the Spirit to do so.

Through our life experiences, there are many people we can reach who won't go to a church building seeking to be saved on their own. During His ministry on Earth and even now from Heaven, Christ calls people from all walks of life. He doesn't make us all over to be the same, prefab Christians, who carry the gospel to the world the same exact way. Christ uses the skills and standings we already have, as well as our cultural frames of reference and the community of people we can touch to draw people to Him.

When Christ called His first disciples, fishermen, He said He would make them fishers of men. These men knew how to fish. They knew where to cast their nets down. They knew when to launch out into deeper waters. They knew when to draw their nets up. They knew how to weave nets and how to repair them. Christ helped them to translate their skill of catching fish to catching men.

There's a wonderful training program for Christians called Fishers of Men. This program teaches individuals how to lead effective bible studies built on the principle men can be caught by Christ. It helps Christians today acquire the skills these fishermen displayed.

Paul was a person with standing. He was learned. He was a man who gave himself wholeheartedly to whatever he did, whether it was persecuting Christians or advancing the cause of Christ. God put Paul's standing and leadership abilities to use. Paul was able to stand before Kings and leaders and proclaim the gospel boldly. Other apostles could have been chosen to do this, but Paul's entire upbringing shaped him into someone who could do it effortlessly.

In the same way, God will use the natural abilities and gifts He gave us to help us win souls to Him. Maybe you are able to develop a connection with someone who loves body piercing and tattoo art because you were into those things at one point. Maybe they will invite you into their community and speak more openly with you than they would with me. Perhaps you will have more in common with someone you meet at a business networking event than someone else would.

Make no mistake: God can use whoever He wants to accomplish whatever He desires. We don't need to wait until we think we are in a good enough position to be used by God. We don't have to discount ourselves or believe our experiences and skills can't be used to bring people to Christ. If we surrender all we are to God, God will use it all to His glory.

We need to get serious about spreading the gospel. We can't get comfortable hunkering down with other Christians who believe like us, think like us, and appear to be living like us. We can't insulate ourselves from opportunities to do the life changing work of spreading the gospel. We may not stand on a stage and proclaim the Word to thousands of women or write bestsellers calling women's hearts back to Christ, but we are to proclaim the good news of the gospel every day with our lives. We are to live it.

If Christ was the Word made flesh and we are to be like Christ, if Christ is alive in us, then we should be a living embodiment of the word ourselves. People should be able to read our lives and be reading God's word.

God gives us all different gifts. Some of us aren't able

to speak or teach as well as others. But we are all alive and therefore capable of living a life glorifying our Father in Heaven. We can all be a light lighting the way to Jesus.

But we have to be willing to shine no matter how dark our surroundings are if we are going to be the light someone follows out of the darkness. We can't dim our light in dark places. People can still stumble and bump into things in a dimly lit room. We can't hide our light under a bushel; we have to give light to the whole room. We can't stay with the other lights and hope those in darkness see us. We need to carry our light into a dark world and be used to seek and save the lost.

In the parable of the lost coin, the woman takes her light and sweeps the house with it, looking for what is lost. What was lost had great value. She didn't stop until she found it. Let God use you the same way. Be the light in His hand He shines into dark corners to find valuable souls lost in the world.

A Second Teaching

Some women are on fire for teaching people who have already been "saved." Other women do a great job getting people involved. They bring people to church for a revival, homecoming, funeral or conferences. They bring people into contact with the Word.

While many people are baptized, sometimes the second teaching the bible admonishes doesn't happen. The initial teaching of the gospel to the lost and baptism are important, but we don't want to be a church who neglects the second teaching the Great Commission commands. If we are going to make others disciples of Christ, we need to teach them the nature of true discipleship.

In order to support the work of discipleship, strong teachers are needed to teach children and new convert women, to share with them the teachings and tenets of Christianity. Teachers must have a strong grasp of and be well versed in the basics of Christianity and how to teach them. We need teachers who are discerning, who know what materials to use when teaching and what methods to use to help us learn. We need teachers who are serious about getting this information rooted in people's hearts.

Whether the teaching style is fun projects and tasks for students or deep discussion, whether the focus is on a specific subject or a passage of scripture, we must treat each lesson as an opportunity to write the word on people's hearts. Whichever part of the spectrum you find yourself on, whether teaching those who don't know God and trying to win souls or working with people who have been baptized on issues arising on their Christian journey, you need to be serious about your role in discipleship.

Both positions require you to be mature. You can't be on milk while teaching people about milk. You can't teach someone something you don't know. If I was baptized last week and I'm leading a bible study this week, I may not know all I need to know to win a soul to Christ. I may not be able to address the things the prospect brings up in the bible study. I need to partner with someone until I know how to teach effectively.

There's an edict in the bible that the older are to teach the younger. I've seen for myself this isn't happening in many of our churches. There are several reasons and rationalizations why this isn't happening:

- younger women aren't interested in the older women teaching them;
- older women don't have the time or energy to teach younger women;
- older women think younger women think they know everything already
- younger women think all the older women do is criticize their generation and talk about how things were in the past.

While all of these excuses may have validity, none of them negate what the Bible instructs us to do.

I don't know many women who are committed to teaching younger women how to love their husbands, be keepers of their home, or any of the practical things outlined in Titus 2. We need to bring back having older women have a forum to teach these things.

Wouldn't it be nice to have classes where women

taught each other how to make different meals or clean a house? Women could teach shortcuts and hacks for completing chores so women could focus more on their families and promoting the cause of Christ in their communities. Younger women could learn how to dress, take care of themselves and protect themselves—all of the intangible things comprising womanhood.

There are several things young women may not learn from their mothers or women in their family if those women aren't in the church. They may not learn about submission. They may not be taught God hates divorce or understand the circumstances in which divorce is allowed. They may not learn how to love their husbands in hard seasons or care for their children in financially trying seasons. They may never learn God is close to the brokenhearted from their biological family, or understand joy comes in the morning. They may not know how to pray for their families or teach their little ones about God the Father, Jesus and the Holy Spirit. They may not be taught to discipline their children without abuse, neglect, or exploitation.

We shouldn't leave women to Google or YouTube for instruction in living lives which honor and glorify God. We shouldn't leave them open to misinformation and worldly teachings on how to get things done.

Teaching younger women may be an area where you can step in and fill a gap sorely in need of filling. I want to encourage you in this, Sister. I'm not here to beat you up about what you haven't been doing. I want to encourage you. You're needed by your sisters. Your wisdom is a necessary component to our life's curriculum. You are called upon to share in the community of Christ, whether the resource is money, time, or life experience and wisdom. Share it with a willing and humble spirit, Sister.

Younger sisters, we need to humble ourselves and get in position to listen. We need to seek out our older sisters and sit at their feet to receive the wisdom they have to share with us. Maybe the older sister isn't going to put her hand on you and take you under her wing without you asking her to teach you. Maybe she won't seek you out. But God will provide you with someone you can learn from. Perhaps you need to take the initiative to seek out a sister who can teach you. Whether a woman reaches out to you or you have to reach out, make the connection, Sister. Your family, present or future, deserves a wife and mother who knows what she is doing and has someone she can go to for wisdom and encouragement.

I'm going to be honest with you. When I began writing Altered before the Altar, I was frustrated and angry with the lack of resources for single women in the church. The focus seemed to be on either how a single woman could get a husband or how she needed to be satisfied with her singleness. The message was don't fornicate. The question was "when are you getting married?"

But I didn't see much teaching on the subject of marriage preparation. I didn't know much about marriage. I knew nothing about being a wife but submission and respecting your husband, and those were just phrases in the bible to me. I felt like someone thrust a parachute in my arms and told me I had to jump out of a plane. With no further instruction, they were trying to shove me out the open door.

What I did next changed my life. I decided if no sister was going to approach me to mentor me or share her wisdom with me, I was going to go to her. I set up interviews with married women about being wives. I sat in living rooms and at dining room tables while women cooked or got children ready for church. I listened while women served food or decorated for events. I met women in their lives and worked alongside them as they told me what to look for in a man, but more importantly, what to develop within myself in preparation for being a wife and mother someday.

I thank God He placed women around me who were willing to sow into me! I am one of those women who didn't learn these things at home. My mother has never been married. Many of my older married relatives never talked about marriage or explained how to make a life with someone. I knew I would be a hot mess in a marriage without some godly wisdom on how to keep a covenant. We need women to meet us in the mess of our lives and show us how to clean it up.

Our different ages, incomes, marital statuses, occupations, and talents, the very things the Enemy uses to divide women, God wants to use to grow women who live lives befitting the title of a daughter of the King. Older women are to teach the younger to do those things outlined in Titus 2 so the Lord isn't blasphemed. So people won't look at us and lie on God. So God's word is proven true.

You know something you can teach me. What you teach me, when I apply it to my life, changes my life. My changed life is seen by someone else who knows I'm a Christian. The person who sees my changed life can now say "God is good. God did an amazing work in Erica."

We have to be committed to mentoring and being mentored. If the church has nothing to say to single women except to get married, the world will speak to them of options and opportunities. If we give our teens and young women nothing but stricture and discouragement, they will find acceptance and freedom in the world. If the church overlooks or sets aside any class of woman, the devil and his demons are ready to entice those women back into the world.

The gospel sets us free. It gives us purpose. It gives us options and opportunities. It gives us a family. It provides a way for us to access a source of unconditional, guaranteed love and acceptance the world can't touch. And we as women play an important part in the Lord's church.

Older women have to teach younger women how to be strong women who add value to their local congregation no matter their marital status. Older women are needed to help young women uncover their gifts and develop them for God's glory. What you have to teach is deeper than how to catch or keep a man: you are teaching women how to live, how to take care of what God blessed them with, and how to represent God to a lost and dying world. God told us what to do; no excuse we could give for not doing His will is sufficient.

Women at War

If we're going to spend time talking about women's roles in discipleship and mentoring one another, we have to talk about the relationships women have with one another. Unfortunately many women are suffering in Leah/Rachel relationships. Yes, we are sisters. We are each a part of the bride of Christ and in the family of God. However, instead of acting as a unified whole expecting to be married to Christ, we act like women fighting over the attentions and affections of the same man.

It seems as if our relationship is based more on competition than cooperation. It's as if we are trying to prove who Christ loves more, blesses more, or gives the most attention. We try to rank ourselves by how many "babies" we birth for the Lord in a spiritual sense. We compete to have or be involved in more ministries. We take pride in being asked to be in charge of certain things. We may rank ourselves by how often we are sought out for our skills and talents. We may seek praise for how many people we help bring to Christ. All in an effort to gain attention and praise, more attention and praise than the next woman.

In the same way Leah and Rachel used having children as a competition, many women today use involvement in ministry and discipleship. They are not beyond piggybacking on someone else's idea and getting residual glory from it just as Rachel and Leah weren't beyond using their servants in their baby war.

If we happen to have something another sister can use, instead of giving it to her, we want to get something out of it as well. Just as Leah asked of her sister when Rachel wanted some of her mandrakes, we ask a sister who needs our help "What can I get out of this? How can I use this to get more attention on what I'm doing for God?"

Living in this transactional manner with other women and seeing all women as competition is exhausting and unfulfilling. It's also not the way Christ prayed for us to be toward one another. Christ spent His last moments before He was taken and crucified praying His followers would be one as He and God are one.

This is a far cry from what is seen in many relationships today. Many of us may have the "doctrine of one" down. We know about the one body, one spirit, one hope, one lord, one faith, and one baptism (Eph. 4:4-5). Yet we forget what Paul says in the preceding verses:

> ¹As a prisoner for the Lord, then, I urge you to live a life worthy of the calling you have received. ²Be completely humble and gentle; be patient, bearing with one another in love. ³Make every effort to keep the unity of the Spirit through the bond of peace. Eph. 4:1-3 NIV

How we miss the point sometimes! The point of highlighting the "ones" in those verses is to show the unity of the Spirit, a unity we are to make every effort to keep. We are to bear one another in love.

Paul also speaks specifically about comparison in Galatians 6. In Galatians 6, Paul talks about how the spiritual are to restore those caught in sin. He also warns us to watch for ourselves and ensure we aren't tempted. He tells us to test our own actions and take pride in ourselves alone, not comparing ourselves with someone else (v. 4).

These scriptures tell us to restore people gently, keeping in mind our own susceptibility to sin (v. 1). They tell us not to compare ourselves with others or take pride in how we stack up against each other. People who live by the Spirit aren't to be in competition with each other. If we are to compare ourselves to anyone, it is to Christ. Christ is our example.

And what does Christ say? Christ tells us to be perfect as God is perfect (Matt. 5:48). Peter quotes the Old Testament and tells us to be holy as God is holy (I Pet 1:15-160 Lev. 11:44, 19:2, 20:7). In both of these instances, if we look at the context of these verses, they are either preceded or followed by admonitions to love others. The greatest command God gives, according to Jesus, is to love the Lord with all our heart, soul and mind. And the second is like unto it: to love our neighbors as ourselves (Matt 22:37-39).

Love is the greatest component of our walk with the Lord when we have been obedient to the truth. Peter says now that you have purified yourselves by obeying the truth so that you have a sincere love for each other, love one another deeply, from the heart (I Pet. 1:22).

Love is the heart changing stuff. Love is the extraordinary work that sets us apart and shows we belong to God. Loving people is our life's work.

The hard part, the part we have to stretch for, is loving our enemies. The hard part shouldn't be to love our sisters.

If I can focus in on the fact God loves my sister and set her apart from the world and claimed her for His own, if I can understand God feels the same way about her as He feels about me, if I can convince myself we are equal in Christ and don't have to jockey for position, maybe I can start moving on to greater victories in Christ and actually doing the work He has for me to do. If I can quiet my flesh and listen to the Spirit God gave me, I can see other women as co-laborers and not competitors. Then I can reap a harvest for the Lord.

Instead of fulfilling Christ's prayer for us to be one, we seek ways to differentiate ourselves from one another. The longer we see each other as competition, the harder it will be to rejoice when others rejoice and mourn when they mourn. We get things all twisted up until we feel awful when our sisters have success and relief when they fail. Sisters, this ought not to be so!

__Women Who Work vs. Women Who Worship__

Sometimes our differences make it difficult to relate to each other. In the story of Mary and Martha related in Luke, Martha is an industrious woman who is busy taking care of the chores and responsibilities of hosting a fellowship in her home. Her sister Mary is more interested in sitting at the feet of Jesus and hearing from Him. They are in the same house, experiencing the same event, but their experiences couldn't be more different.

There are some women in our congregations who may feel like they are doing more than their fair share of the practical stuff. They have boots on the ground doing all the behind the scenes work: they're helping in the kitchen during fellowships. They are there to set up before events and to tear down afterward. They make sure everything is running smoothly. They keep glasses of lemonade filled and little hands and faces wiped clean. If someone is sick or bereaved, these are the sisters who round everyone up and organize prayer chains and visitation schedules. When someone has a child or is getting married, these sisters plan the shower. If there is work to be done, these sisters do it.

Then there are the sisters who come and worship. They soak in the word being preached or taught. They luxuriate in the fellowship taking place. They may be in a season where they aren't overly involved in the mechanics of a woman's role in the church. They're coming to sit at Jesus' feet and take in every word. They are intent on hearing what He has to say to them at this moment.

The women who are working can become frustrated with the women who are worshipping. Working women may feel worshipping women aren't carrying their share of the load. Worshipping women may feel working women are missing God in all their busyness. Both feel justified in their position.

Christ says both Martha's and Mary's positions are needed. We all go through seasons. We won't always be working and helping out. We won't always be led to sit and enjoy the fellowship without participating in the work inherent in hosting an event.

Balance and understanding are needed in our relationships with one another. Everyone will not work or worship as I would when I would. We are to encourage and exhort one another, not berate each other.

What God Wants for Women

If Leah and Rachel, and Mary and Martha, are examples of unhealthy relationships between women, the relationship between Mary, the mother of Jesus, and her cousin Elizabeth is an example of a fulfilling relationship between women. Elizabeth is an older woman who has been barren up to this point in time and Mary is a young virgin. They couldn't be more opposite. But they are related by blood and both fully given to being servants of God. They are committed to birthing what God has put in them to birth.

Elizabeth receives Mary when she comes to visit her in light of the promise God has given to both of them (Luke 1:39-45). They share in each other's joy. Mary stays with Elizabeth for months (v. 56).

These two women are going through this process together. They are preparing to birth children who will play key roles in the plan of God to pave the way for man's salvation. Instead of feeling envious of each other or letting their differences separate them, Mary and Elizabeth spend their pregnancies together. They support one another and affirm their destinies to each other by the Spirit in a beautiful picture of female solidarity.

Relationships between Christian women are an important dynamic to discuss when talking about getting serious about who we are in Christ and where we are as women. We cannot grow in Christ if we are not following His command to love one another. Building loving relationships helps us grow out of covetousness, comparison, and competition. If I love my sister, I want the best for her. It teaches me to deny myself and my desires and to seek after God's will.

The great thing about growing in our relationship with God is the grace, mercy and love He fills us with to overflowing flows out into every other area of our lives. Growing women love each other. They are gracious to one another. They show each other mercy. They forgive quickly. They won't stay stuck in hurt feelings or distrust; they move forward in faith.

CHAPTER FIFTEEN

On a Mission, But Out of Position

So when you've had difficult seasons or times in your life, how have you been able to stay focused, if you were, or if you weren't, what knocked you off track?

Sis. Zelda Jones: Accepting His will, knowing that I really can't do anything. I am leaning on Him, trusting Him…I don't have the wherewithal to impact change in a way that makes me the one that's in control, because I'm not in control. I just give it to God. It's not easy. There are many times where I have felt like I was going to jump in there and do this and do that. Regrettably I have done that and it's just a mess. So I just give it to the Lord.

Sometimes the hardest person to redirect is the person who thinks they are doing what God told them to do. This is the case with Saul. Saul tells Samuel "I did what God told me to do. I completed the mission God sent me on." Samuel corrects Saul. He reminds Saul of what God actually asked him to do and showed Saul how he'd done differently, but Saul insists he's completed the mission satisfactorily.

But Saul was appointed by God to lead the people. He's only stepping in and doing what needs to be done. They're going into battle and if they want the Lord to go with them, *someone* needed to offer a burnt offering and a peace offering. Since Samuel wasn't present, Saul took it upon himself to do so (Sam. 13:8-10).

Saul was correct in his assumption someone needed to offer a burnt offering and a peace offering to the Lord. The problem is God called Samuel to this office, not Saul. Saul is not the person who is supposed to do this. Alternatively, when God tells Saul specifically to utterly destroy all the Amalekites have and slay all the people, Saul fails to do so. Saul goes above and beyond what he is supposed to do in both of these scenarios, yet he somehow manages to bungle his assignment while meddling in others'.

As Christian women, there are several opportunities for us to make the same error as Saul did. There are places God wants someone to go and things He wants someone to do, but those things aren't getting done. Many women see this and immediately jump in to "fill the gap." Yet God didn't designate them for the position. The women who step in often know they aren't designated for the task, but the task must be done and no one else is doing it.

The fact "no one else is doing it" doesn't give us the license to do it. How many of us are in places we shouldn't be in, doing things we shouldn't be doing because "somebody has to do it"? How many of us say to ourselves, "I'm going to be Super Christian and sacrifice. I'm going to pull up my bootstraps and fill in where I need to fill in"? Yet no one told us, least of all God, to be over there doing that—nobody. We expect to be blessed because we are doing God's work, but we are not doing God's will, which can be a completely different thing.

What both of these stories illustrate is other people are important. Things must be done decently and in order. We need everyone to be working in the capacity God has for them to work in order to function as a body. But just because someone isn't in position when we want them to be in position, it doesn't mean we should step in and take over for them. When we are rebuked or checked for overstepping, we may try to justify our actions by saying "someone had to do it" or "I needed to do something." But this isn't the Lord talking. This is our impatience and maybe even our bossy/manipulative nature rearing its ugly head.

Instead of being still and waiting on God, instead of being where we're supposed to be, doing what we're supposed to be doing, we are in someone else's position and wondering why we aren't growing. We never stop to think: If I'm filling in for someone else, if I'm where someone else should be, who's doing what I'm supposed to be doing? Aren't I doing the very thing I'm upset about in the first place by not being in position myself? Am I holding up progress somewhere else the way I perceived progress was being held up in this area? Is someone else depending on me to do what God told me to do while I'm out of position?" What are you doing here? Sometimes we're in the right place but not in the right position. We are where we are meant to be, but we aren't doing what we are designated to do in that space.

Sometimes what we're supposed to be doing is waiting. We're supposed to be being still. We're not supposed to be *doing* anything. We're just waiting. We're looking expectantly to God to do something, to provide something, or to send someone, and that's OK if it's in the will of God. We don't have to be responsible for moving everything forward. Sometimes we can't move anything forward. If we aren't being spiritual and looking at things with spiritual eyes, we are not going to see how out of step we are with God when we try to go ahead of Him.

There are consequences to the decisions we make and the things we do when we start acting out of the will of God. We see this in the story of Uzziah (II Chr. 26). Uzziah started out doing that which was right in the sight of the Lord. He sought the Lord (v. 4-5). But then Uzziah got beside himself and transgressed against the Lord by going into the temple to burn incense on the altar of incense (v. 16). Some of the priests came and stood up to him, telling him the priest were the ones designated to burn incense and he would receive no honor from the Lord for acting out of position (v17-18). He became angry with them. In the midst of him being angry with them, he broke out with leprosy (v. 19). Because of his leprosy, Uzziah was unable to go to the house of the Lord and was separated from society. Even in death, he was separated. He was buried in a burial field belonging to the kings but outside of the royal tomb.

Sometimes we think God is telling us to do something, and instead of checking, we just do what we feel we need to do. This causes us to be out of position and we are often beaten back. This happened to Joshua and the children of Israel in the battle of Ai. During the fall of Jericho, Achan sinned by taking a robe, silver, and gold and hiding them in his tent (Josh. 7:21). When the people tried to move forward and take the tiny city of Ai, they were killed and chased from before the gates. The people's hearts melted because of this defeat. We can read this and wonder why God punished all the people for Achan's sin. But we must realize two things: a) there were people who knew what Achan had done who didn't say anything and b) Joshua and the others went ahead with their battle plans without consulting God.

Neither Joshua nor anyone else ever consulted with God until after they were routed back by the people of Ai. After they were routed back, then there was the tearing of clothes, wearing ashes and sackcloth, and asking God what he was doing. They didn't consult Him when they decided they weren't going to send everyone to fight Ai. They thought they could deal with Ai themselves. They didn't consult God on how many people to send. They didn't check to make sure they were right with God. They didn't consecrate themselves. They assumed they were on good terms with God instead of communicating with Him. God could have told them before they left there was sin in their midst.

It's easy on this side of it to assign blame or see Achan or the people as more or less fallible, but the point is all were punished. When there is sin in the midst, God doesn't go with you. While it is easy for us to judge who is at fault in situations like this, we have trouble seeing our fault when we do the same thing.

We'll have a victory--we get a promotion or a raise or get married and we think the next thing, the next battle, will be easy. We can put it on auto-pilot. We don't have to put all our energy into this little task. God's already got this. God is in control. Yet we haven't consulted God. We didn't ask God. We aren't interested in what God has to say. God has already "shown up and shown out" on our behalf. We think we have God's favor and God is with us now because He was in the past. We take His involvement as a given when we need to continue to seek Him. This was Uzziah's mistake. It was Joshua and the children of Israel's mistake. It is often our mistake.

We don't constantly seek His will. We're not constantly asking Him. We think God's just supposed to make things happen for us. If stuff doesn't happen for us, we don't understand what the problem is. We need to have continuous communication with God.

We need to be concerned about moving forward without God's blessing. We can't rush blindly through life with no idea where we're going or what we're doing. We can't expect to do whatever we want in life and think God is going to come through and fix everything we destroy in our wake.

Throughout their history, the children of Israel rebelled against going where God sent them. They fought to stay where they were. They refused to move ahead. They sought to go back. They tried to go forward when God told them not to. They refused to listen to His messengers and go where He told them to go at every turn. And it always led to their destruction.

Be open to God's leading, Sister. Don't close your ears to His voice. Don't take the attitude the Israelites took with God, where you don't want to talk to Him and you don't want Him to talk to you. Don't be the sister who thinks God just needs to bless some stuff in your life and then go about His business and think you're getting somewhere. God doesn't accept just anything. God isn't going to bless everything. Don't get stuck in stagnation because you insist on being out of place. Grow in your garden, Sister. Stop looking at everyone else's garden and trying to tell them what they need to do to grow bigger and better crops and pay attention to what God is trying to do with you.

CHAPTER SIXTEEN

When we are growing in Christ, we should be growing loving relationships with other Christians. Loving is the greatest commandment—to love the Lord, our neighbors, and other Christians. We are supposed to show love to others by giving of our resources, visiting them in their afflictions, praying for them, feeding and clothing them, and showing them the love of God.

But sometimes, love hurts. Loving people isn't always this beautiful picture of selfless service which elicits gratitude and praise. Sometimes our help isn't welcomed or appreciated. Sometimes we are ill-treated or abused for our offer of help. Sometimes when we extend the right hand of fellowship, we get bitten.

If we are spiritual, we are tasked with restoring those overtaken in a fault (Gal. 6:1). In my mind, this looked like a beautiful renaissance painting where I reach down to a fallen sister who is reaching up to me in gratitude. But not everyone overtaken in a fault appreciates our attempts to restore them. Every sister doesn't set out to restore another in the right spirit. We aren't always prepared for the temptations inherent in restoration, nor the opposition we are met with from the one we are trying to restore.

One example of an effort to save someone resulting in mistreatment is found in the story of Balaam's donkey. We've already discussed Balaam himself in "Deaf, Dumb and Blind," but what about the donkey who saved his life? What can we learn from her actions to have a better perspective on helping our sisters?

Balaam's donkey cannot speak or justify her actions initially. She cannot give an account of herself and why she is doing what she is doing. Unbeknownst to Balaam, his donkey is seeing what he cannot and is operating on what she sees. Balaam becomes increasingly frustrated with his donkey when she turns aside, presses too close to walls, and sits down beneath him. He beats her repeatedly for what he sees as her insubordination. God opens the donkey's mouth and Balaam's eyes before Balaam can understand what his donkey has done for him.

As Christians, sometimes we see things other people don't. Our lives are guided and moved by God to work around and through things other people don't even realize are there. Whenever you are operating on spiritual knowledge, there is the potential for the worldly or unspiritual to misunderstand or attack you. Even when what we are doing is to the saving of someone's soul, when they can't see the danger, we can be mistreated, talked about, and scorned. Our actions aren't always going to be understood or appreciated by the people we are trying to save.

There are three different things Balaam's donkey does before her mouth and Balaam's eyes are opened. Studying her responses in depth will give us a few key things to consider when we are mistreated when operating on what we see by faith, especially when trying to restore someone.

1. **She turns aside** (v. 23). When Balaam starts out on his journey, the angel of the Lord stands in the way to oppose Balaam. The angel's sword is drawn and ready. Instead of continuing moving toward him, the donkey turns aside. Sometimes we are called upon to take someone off the path they are intent on traveling down. Notice the donkey doesn't buck Balaam off or turn around; instead, she turns aside. It's the path of least resistance. She is smote for her efforts and turned back onto the path. Our attempts to redirect someone may be met with force. We may be abused when we try to

help. It's up to us to decide how we will respond to this abuse.

2. **She pressed close to the wall** (v. 24-25). The next time Balaam's donkey sees the angel of the Lord, the angel is standing in the path of the vineyards between two walls. This space is too small for her to turn aside or give the angel a wide berth. She has to press close to the wall to get around him. In the process, she crushes Balaam's foot and receives another beating. This happens in situations where we do or say something for someone else's good and inadvertently injure them or cause them pain. They may be upset about the little pain they received when there was a bigger pain we helped them avoid. Open rebuke is better than hidden love (Prov. 27:5), but it still stings. Plucking out an eye to save the rest of the body is a wise decision (Matt. 5:29), but it still hurts and handicaps. When we have to say or do things which may injure a part to save the whole, we need to be sure what we are doing is profitable to the whole, and we must be ready to be hurt in return.

3. **She lay down underneath him** (v. 26-27). The third time the angel of the Lord stands in the way to oppose the donkey, he stands in a narrow space with no way for her to get around him. The donkey's only choice is to lay down beneath him. Sometimes when someone is depending on us to get where they are trying to go, we have to refuse to go forward with them. We have to resist the command to go forward. There's no way to get around what's in front of them. This is the only time the bible specifies Balaam beat the donkey with his staff. This is a more aggressive smiting than the previous ones. When we have to take a hard stance against someone, we are going to be met with this level of fierce opposition.

Balaam's donkey finds herself in narrower and

narrower spaces where it is less and less possible to avoid the angel of the Lord. When someone who once walked with the Lord begins walking opposed to Him, it is going to become more and more difficult to avoid divine correction. The donkey is loyal to Balaam and attempts to save his life despite repeated mistreatment.

This should be the main takeaway for us. When we care about a sister and her eternal soul, we will endure a little persecution or mistreatment trying to save her. When the time comes, God will provide the sister with the understanding of what has been done for her. We cannot predict the outcome of our efforts, but we can be hopeful our sister will be saved from the dangerous path she's traveling.

CHANGING SEASONS

Fruit or Flower?

God's people are described in agricultural and gardening terms numerous times in the bible. The bible is filled with references to sowing, reaping, harvest, trees, vines and fruit. But there are few references to flowers.

Flowers are often referred to in conjunction with the temporary. Flowers wither, fade, and die. They are attractive, but they don't last.

In nature, many plants and trees flower before they produce fruit or nuts. The flowers serve a function, but they are not the crop; the fruit is.

Fruit is a renewable resource. It contains the seed of life and ensures the continuation of the species. There is no question of the fruit's utility.

It is the same in our lives. Like flowers, physical beauty fades. Our youth fades. It is the fruit of the spirit that lasts. We know we must bear fruit. But what purpose do flowers serve in the Christian life?

This entire book up to this point has been focused on growth and getting us to grow. Growth is an essential component of any living thing. We want our relationship with God to be living and growing.

But what exactly are we growing? Are we growing flowers or fruit?

In the parable of the sower, seeds were planted in all but one scenario. Some plants were choked by weeds and thorns and others were burned up. Only one flourished. We've planted seeds and things have started to grow, but is our plant sustainable? Will it be choked out or burned up? Will it be a flower, beautiful but destined to wither and fade? Or will it bear fruit?

Flowers aren't bad. As I said before, many plants flower before they produce fruit. The flowering of these plants and trees serves a purpose. The flowers have utility. The point is not to become so focused on the beauty of the flower, we miss the opportunity to bear fruit.

We need to be able to tell whether the growth in our lives is flower or fruit. We need to know its function or purpose to determine what we should spend our time cultivating. Let's look at some characteristics and truths about flowers and fruit to help us identify what we are growing and how to make the most of whatever season we are in.

1. **Flowers are not the focus.** The flowers in our lives get us by in the beginning or help us to become established. They prove we aren't barren. They are a sign of life. They brighten our visage and keep us from appearing bare. But flowers are not the end goal. Just because you have flowers on your tree, it doesn't mean you can sit back and rest. Those flowers aren't going to last. They're going to die. And when they die, you will need to produce the fruit the flower promises.

2. **But flowering is important.** Flowers provide the opportunity for cross-pollination. They attract bees, which carry pollen from one flower to another. In other words, flowers bring the potential for you to be exposed to what's happening elsewhere. You are exposed to what's helping others grow. The flowers of life can be a point of contact with those in the world as well. Someone can see what you are doing or how you seem to be growing and they can be attracted to you. People can be encouraged or hear the gospel because of your flowers.

3. **Flowers attract bees just by being flowers.**

The beauty of a flower is it doesn't have to work at attracting bees. When Jesus refers to our basic needs, he invites us to look at the lilies of the field. Even Solomon wasn't arrayed as well as they are (Matt. 6:28-29). Jesus said if we will seek Him first, things like clothing and food will be added unto us (Matt. 6:33). If we concentrate on growing fruit, we will flower, and if we flower, the bees will come.

4. **No one has to tell you when to bloom or when to produce fruit.** If you are planted where you're supposed to be planted and your roots are working the way they should, you will produce a crop. People may be able to identify the season by what they see, but they don't determine the season. Only God gives the increase.

5. If you are bare right now, take heart. **Being bare doesn't mean you are barren.** It doesn't mean you will never again produce fruit. Trees are often bare between flowering and growing fruit. Even if people can't see any fruit from the outside, it doesn't mean you are unproductive. Give forth fruit in YOUR season, according to God's timing. Don't rush to have the promise without the performance. Remember, Christ cursed the fig tree with the nice leaves which looked good for fruit but didn't have any figs on it (Matt. 21:18-19).

6. How does a bare tree in the winter show forth God's glory? By being bare. By resting from producing fruit, flowers, or leaves. **You have to allow yourself to rest in seasons of rest, Sister.** Everything but humans understands the need for rest. Certain animals hibernate for the winter; others migrate to a better climate. Plants stop growing but are still living and storing up until spring, when they will bud again. Prepare appropriately to rest. Rest is a gift of God. The below ground work of being broken wide open and dying to self that allows us to come up out of the ground is important. You would be amazed at the

root system of even the simplest plants. Their root systems sustain them and carry vital nutrients throughout their bodies. Don't be afraid to cover yourself and focus inward. Let God break some things and grow some things nobody else knows about right now. They may never know about it! They may only see what it supports and wonder where you get your strength.

7. **Saplings are flexible.** They will bend under pressure, but they won't break. Even big trees with deep roots can bend without breaking under intense pressure. Be flexible in the storm. Bend but don't break. Take the good and use it, and withstand the rest.

8. **Your fruit isn't just about you.** A tree doesn't eat its own fruit. The fruit is the vehicle by which the seed, the life giving portion of the tree, is spread. Our fruit should have the seed of the word in it, to grow even more trees for the Lord.

9. **Fruit is for others.** Just as animals eat fruit, the fruit of the spirit is something we can use to nourish others.

10. **You don't need to show off your fruit.** Those who are hungry will seek it out.

11. **Fruit is a renewable resource we have.** Giving of our fruit to others isn't going to create scarcity for us. As long as we are connected to the vine, we will produce fruit.

12. **Whether it is a flower or a fruit, growth is good.** Don't waste the short season of blossoming looking for the fruit. Enjoy the season you are in, whether it's a season of being bare, flowering, producing fruit, or harvesting the fruit.

CHAPTER SEVENTEEN

The Miracle Worker

> Miracle: an unusual or wonderful event that is believed to be caused by the power of God; an extraordinary event manifesting divine intervention in human affairs.
>
> Miraculous: very wonderful or amazing like a miracle; of the nature of a miracle; suggesting a miracle: marvelous; working or able to work miracles.
>
> Wonderful: extremely good, exciting wonder, unusually good.

Our goal as Christians is to be like Jesus. Jesus' life on earth is an example to us of what our lives were intended to be. He lived a perfect life before us so we would know how to live before our Father in Heaven and be pleasing and acceptable to Him.

Christians believe those who were baptized into Christ have put on Christ (Gal. 3:27). We believe the old man was crucified with Christ (Rom. 6:6). As Paul says, it's no longer I who live but Christ liveth in me (Gal. 2:20). We believe the same power used to raise Christ from the dead is operating in us right now, according to Ephesians 1:19-20 and Romans 8:11. We believe we can follow in the footsteps of the Savior. But how many of us believe we can perform miracles and do the miraculous in Christ?

I hear people proclaiming they aren't miracle workers every day. Usually the individual saying this has been asked to do something they feel like they can't do within the specified timeframe with the resources at their disposal. Often it is either too late to fit the request in or they need higher authority or permission not readily available. Whatever the reason, they feel as if they are not able to do what the person is asking of them.

Can we do the miraculous in Christ, or is this too big a request? Can Christians be miraculous and do the miraculous like Jesus did?

The simple dictionary definition of a miracle is an unusual or wonderful event believed to be caused by the power of God. The adjective miraculous is used to describe the ability to work miracles. The question of whether or not we can be miraculous may be better stated this way: can we be used by God to do something extremely good through His power?

Of course we can! If we believe we can be used by God to do something extremely good through His power, we can do the miraculous today. It isn't a matter of capability but availability.

We may not be able to perform the physical miracles of restoring sight, raising the dead, or healing the sick, but we can perform acts just as miraculous for the people around us. We can replicate the positive impact Jesus had on the lives of those He performed miracles for during His ministry if we are willing to let God use us to bless others.

Miracles weren't magic tricks but manifestations of the power of God performed for a specific purpose. The purpose of a miracle in Jesus' ministry on Earth was to provide validation of Jesus' claim He was the Son of God. The miracles the apostles performed were confirmation of the gospel they preached. Miracles provide recognition of God and confirmation of His word. Miracles proclaim "God is here! Freedom is here! Redemption is here! Salvation is here! The answer is here!" The proper response to a miracle is either to confess Jesus to be the Christ, the Messiah, or to praise God.

Do you know what else is supposed to be seen by men and cause them to glorify our Father in Heaven? Our good works (Matt. 5:16). Our light is supposed to shine before men. The things we do should cause people to glorify God in the same way miracles do.

In every instance of Jesus or His disciples performing a miracle, the need is apparent. Miracles weren't magic tricks performed for applause; they were addressing the needs of the people. In the same way, the miracles we can perform today should address the needs of those around us who need to know God is here.

How do we perform miracles today? Without the miraculous power Jesus and His apostles commanded, how do we accomplish the extremely good? What power is at our disposal to make miracles happen?

The Real Miracle Worker

The members of the church at Corinth coveted the spiritual gifts they thought would bring them more notoriety and esteem. However, Paul encourages them to desire the more useful gifts which weren't temporary in nature. His dissertation on the greatest gift is a familiar passage to many of us.

Many quote I Corinthians 13 at weddings without realizing the true intent of these verses. Paul declares the gifts of speaking in tongues, being able to prophesy, and having knowledge would cease to exist, but our ability to love will never pass away (v. 8-10). Faith, hope and love abide to this day (v. 13).

We've spent a great deal of this book cultivating faith to promote growth in Christ. But in order to get to the next level, we have to cultivate our love for one another. Love is the greatest gift God gave us; loving the greatest commandment He gave. It's also the key to being miraculous, or changing lives to the glory of God.

Anything we do for God or man not done with love is useless, even good things. The source of the love we work from is the fact God first loved us. We love others out of the love He's shown us. The example of God's great love for us is what we use to dispense love to others. Without the foundation or basis of love, nothing else we do matters.

The first three verses of I Corinthians 13 make this concept abundantly clear. It doesn't matter if you can speak every language and communicate with all people; if you don't have love, you are just a noisemaker, a distraction from what's really important (v. 1). Paul says a person with the gift of prophesy, special knowledge, or faith that can move mountains without love is nothing. What you know doesn't make you any more important, special or blessed than anyone else (v. 2). In verse three, Paul moves to good deeds and sacrifice. If you give all without a heart of love, you don't gain anything. It profits you nothing.

In summary, without love, you say nothing, you gain nothing and you are nothing. Forget doing something miraculous; you aren't even average if you aren't doing it in love.

These verses give examples of all the gifts the Corinthians coveted. These were the spiritual gifts they placed the most value in. Not only does Paul say these gifts are useless without love, He also states they will cease and fail at some point. After that which was perfect came, there would be no more need for prophesy, speaking in tongues, or special knowledge of God. Since we have the perfect law of liberty, in which is recorded all prophecies up to the end of the world and into eternity, we have no need of these temporary gifts.

But faith, hope, and love are still here with us. These are the gifts of the spirit we must work from. And love is the greatest one.

With love, we can do miraculous things. We can do what is outside of someone's ability to do for themselves. We can provide life changing, life altering sustenance at just the right moment—when the individual doesn't see a solution and is about to give up.

Most of the miracles Jesus did were for people at this stage. They have a small amount of faith they're holding on to when Christ comes and changes everything.

The miraculous changes lives, not just temporary circumstances. Even if the miracle addresses a momentary need, the experience will change the lives of the recipients forever.

Do we have the ability to change lives? Yes, if we are willing to let go of everything we have or want and allow God to take over and use us to change lives.

I'm going to make and validate some bold statements here. I believe we have the ability to raise people from the dead, give sight to the blind, open the ears of the deaf, give the lame the power to walk, feed the masses, and heal the sick today. In fact, scripture calls us to do just that. We have the ability to completely change the quality of the lives of those around us who are suffering. God will allow us to do these things if we surrender to His will.

We need to get serious about the miraculous and the "impossible." We need to get serious about thinking bigger and being used for more. When I think about the person of Jesus, the miracles He performed, the ways in which He impacted people's lives, and the areas of their lives He impacted, I realize I limit the power of Christ in me when I'm not willing to give myself over to be used for more. We can impact people in the areas Christ did if we allow God to use us.

People chase what they think is miraculous. They would love to be able to put their hands on someone and restore sight, or multiply food. But loving each other is the truly miraculous gift. And we all have the ability to use this gift. It's amazing how little we have to do to be a miracle to somebody else.

Let's go through the different types of miracles Jesus performed and see how we can do the miraculous today. Keep in mind the definition of a miracle—an unusual or wonderful event caused by the power of God.

- Turn water into wine (John 2:1-11). Jesus performed this miracle at a wedding when they ran out of wine. In this time of celebration, Jesus secretly helped the servants keep the guests happy. We can help a work, a ministry, or someone performing a specific job to God's glory. We can pitch in behind the

scenes so others can rejoice and celebrate out front. The people who need to see our work will, and God will be glorified.
- Feed the five thousand (John 6:1-13). We can feed people in a variety of ways. We can volunteer at a food bank or homeless shelter, bring a dish to a fellowship meal or a grieving family, or invite someone to a meal. We can feed hungry sinners the bread of life, the word of God. We may not be able to feed five thousand people at once, but we can impact lives in our sphere of influence to the glory of God.
- Heal lepers (Matt. 8:1-4). Lepers were people who were isolated from society because of their illness. Jesus wasn't afraid to reach out to them and heal them. We as believers are tasked with loving the rejects of our society and introducing them to Christ. We should be birthing them into a spiritual family, a community in which they are included and accepted.
- Give hearing to the deaf (Mark 7:31-37). How then shall they call on him in whom they have not believed? And how shall they believe in him of whom they have not heard? And how shall they hear without a preacher? ...So then faith cometh by hearing and hearing the word of God. Rom. 10:14, 17. We can give hearing to the deaf by sharing the word of God with them and bringing them to Christ. The preceding verse states whosoever shall call upon the name of the Lord shall be saved. All we are doing is pointing the person to Jesus.
- Heal the sick. We can visit the sick. We can make sure the things they need done get done and they get to the places they need to go. We can bring them food and make sure they take medications. We can aid the healing process

by the way we care for them. At the very least, we can be there with them and be someone they can talk to, which has been proven to help people heal.
- Raise the dead (John 11:1-45). We can raise someone dead in sin to life. We can give people a new life by introducing them to Christ and His word and the power of His word when we are obedient to His word and being led by His spirit.

Every single one of the miracles above is to show the glory and love of God to all men. Remember, God is love and love is the greatest spiritual gift we have. Through loving people well, we can introduce to some and present to others the Great Physician, the One who can perform physical miracles as well as spiritual ones. When Christ comes into someone's life, He does the undeniably miraculous. He changes everything!

Our Miraculous God

God's love for us set the miraculous in motion from before the foundation of the world (Eph. 1:4, 2:9). There are several times in scripture when Jesus performed miracles and told the recipient to tell no one. In some instances this was because it wasn't yet time for His ministry to be known. Even though His ministry hadn't officially started, Jesus performed miracles out of compassion and love for people.

Yes, His ability to perform miracles was a sign that He was the Messiah, the one sent by God to redeem the world, but His performance of miracles was out of His great love and compassion for man. He wanted to help people. He wanted to end suffering. His whole mission here, His death on the cross, was to conquer sin and death, to restore us, to provide a way for us to have a relationship with God.

If we could accept God loves us, that He is love, and recognize the miraculous things He does for us each and every day, we wouldn't struggle so much with the concept of the miraculous. The power of God is still bringing about unusual and wonderful events today, and we get to be a part of the process if we are willing to accept the love God gives to us and let it overflow into the lives of those around us.

How do we become serious about doing the miraculous? There are three things we need to do in order to participate with Christ in doing the miraculous:
1. **We have to be able to see the needs people have.** We can't close ourselves off and hide in our little bubble. The people Jesus healed on earth weren't the people who were His disciples and followed Him. They were part of the crowd who gathered when He came to a place and dissipated when He left. They were people who happened to be in a certain place at a certain time. They were even people who sought Him out in faith to do the miraculous for them. But they weren't devotees. He was spreading a message of faith, hope, and love to those who were lost. The people we can provide the miraculous for aren't always going to be in the pew next to us. The lives we can really effect may be the ones we avert our eyes from and speak curtly to as we are rushing about our day. The ones we really don't want to be bothered with. The ones we have to get our hands dirty to handle. If you want to do the miraculous work of our big brother Jesus, pray for God to open your eyes to the needs of those around you. Pray for compassion for people and to see the similarities between yourself and people who would otherwise be labeled outcasts or thought of as less than. You cannot touch those you refuse to see. We have to get real about who we are called to serve. Those who are healthy don't need a physician. Those who can meet every challenge and defy all the odds don't need a miracle. Once God opens your eyes to the needs around you, you can become overwhelmed. You

will see more needs than you could ever meet. Ask God to show you which needs you should attempt to address. Really seek His will and not your comfort zone.

2. **You have to be willing to interact with disease, pain or grief.** When I see someone is emotional, upset, or in some way visibly struggling, my instinct is to turn away. We think it's impolite to look at someone who is going through something. We "give them a moment to collect themselves." When people have disabilities, we may avoid interacting with them or use degrading and limiting language about them and with them in conversation. One of the things I learned working with developmentally disabled people and exceptional students is everyone deserves to be treated as if they matter. If we are willing to get in the muck and mire of someone else's experience, we can do much more than we imagine. This may require some work on our part. This may require learning about diseases and treatments. This may require learning different communication styles and committing to continuing to try until you can understand what the person is trying to say. It may involve the hard work of being silent and present for someone else. We will have to expose ourselves to hurts and afflictions we can't possibly treat, let alone cure. Sometimes we are going to mess this work up, whatever it is. But we don't have to be perfect; we just have to be willing.

3. **We have to be willing to touch them. Jesus touched people.** He put His hands on them. He didn't just tell them to get it together. Every now and then He spoke to people and they were healed, but for the most part, His miracles were hands on. If we are going to perform miracles, we have to be willing to

touch people. I don't mean physically. I mean we have to get close to them. In order to touch someone, you have to be close and your hands have to be empty. This is what we are really to do; to touch people. To feed, to clothe, to dress wounds, and to be a presence showing them they are not alone. When James speaks about faith without works being dead, he gives the example of someone saying to a brother or sister who is naked or hungry "go in peace. Be warmed and filled." It's a wonderful sentiment, but it doesn't accomplish anything. It doesn't profit the person anything if we don't do what's needful to the body (James 2:14-17).

We need the endowment of Christ, the power of Christ, Christ's strength within us. We need Him to strengthen us and go before us. We can do nothing without Him. With us, we can fail, but it is impossible for God to fail. His love is our driving force. It both compels and propels us.

If we aren't operating out of the strength, love and concern of God which was shown to us or the example of Christ, then we can't affect change. We can't change our lives or anyone else's. Operating from any other source, we become like the scribes and Pharisees. We make rules and establish traditions in an attempt to replace what is irreplaceable. Never exchange the truth of God's ability to work miracles for the lie He no longer specializes in the impossible.

CHANGING SEASONS

Success & the Serious Sister

> [W]hen I was younger I used to yearn for the spotlight...I wanted to be Halle Berry, Oprah Winfrey... I really really did...but I don't think that was God's plan for me...And now that I'm older, I'm more willing to lean more toward what His plans are, what He wants vs. what I want...For me success will be when I pass away, He says "well done, my good and faithful servant." That's the only success I want. ~Sis. Zelda Jones

Most of this book, and most of the teachings and sermons we hear on the Christian journey, deals with how to grow in times of hardship. The focus is usually on how to count it all joy when you go through trials and tribulations. But what about when you have attained some level of success? What does success look like on our Christian journey? What are the landmarks we should be looking for to identify if we are on the road to true success?

First, let's make it personal and specific: What is successful to you? Can success be achieved in your lifetime? What would have to change in order for you to be successful?

Here's the Instagram/social media obsessed culture of today's version of the road to success: get up before and stay up later than everyone else. Grind. Hustle. Have multiple hustles and streams of income. Chase money and connections leading to money. Never be satisfied. Always keep pushing. You're not successful unless you own your own business, set your own hours, and control your paycheck. If you feel overwhelmed by all you have to do, remember when you didn't have the opportunities you have now and KEEP PUSHING.

The dictionary defines success a couple different ways. The first is getting or achieving wealth, fame, or respect. You're not successful until the right people know who you are, respect what you do and pay you well to do it. This narrow view of success leads to chasing an ideal you can never catch. Once you "achieve" success, you are in the untenable position of having to keep succeeding. You are constantly compared to up and comers. You have to keep accomplishing bigger and better things to stay respected and famous. You have to build on your wealth while being a few bad investments away from ruin. One wrong step can send you crashing back to earth and obscurity. You can be famous one day and forgotten the next. You can be wealthy today and lose it all tomorrow. It's an untenable position, a balancing act where any wrong move can send you crashing back to earth and obscurity. The feeling of satisfaction is fleeting; there's always more to do and more to lose.

Another dictionary definition of success is the correct or desired result of an attempt. This is a much more attainable goal. You either get a correct or desired result or you don't. The catch, though, is sometimes the correct result isn't the desired result. In other words, success may not look like we think it should. For example, in the book Boy Meets Girl: Say Hello to Courtship, the author describes a successful courtship as one in which two people make an informed decision about whether or not to get married. Whether the answer is to get married or to separate, they have achieved their aim.

Most people don't view success this way. They view success as getting what they want out of life. This is why there is a bigger focus on growing in difficult seasons. Many of us need the perspective or paradigm shift to see the success coming to fruition in more challenging times. Our inability to see how successful we are, right now, right where we are, holds us back from being more fruitful. Success builds on success.

Before we can focus on growing while successful, we must grow success. We have to understand God's definition of success and view our lives in light of this. Learning biblical characteristics and principles of success will help us to recognize success in our lives and strive to build on the successes we see.

The Seed of Success

The first principle of success we must learn is **success takes time.** Tom Clancy said an overnight success is ten years in the making. There is no such thing as an overnight success. God isn't on our timetable or confined by our constructs of time. To us, it may seem like it's taking forever for us to see progress or we're falling behind, when to God we are right on schedule.

A good example of this is God's promise to Abraham. God promised Abraham his seed would be as innumerable as the sands of the sea. But the realization of this promise started off small. By the time Abraham has a child, he and his wife are well past childbearing years. Sarah is 90 when she gives birth to Isaac! Abraham has two sons, but only Isaac is part of the promise. He has to believe this one child will somehow be multiplied in future generations to be innumerable. Isaac has two sons as well, Jacob and Esau. Esau doesn't inherit any of the promise. He loses his birthright and his blessing. So we're still with one. Jacob is blessed to have 12 children. Those 12 are fruitful and multiply. By the time we get to the events in Exodus, they estimate over 2.2 million Israelites left Egypt.

This growth took a long time. The Israelites were in bondage in Egypt for 400 years. Even though the people were suffering oppression and Pharaoh tried to genocide them by killing all their male babies, there was still outrageous growth. God was responsible for their growth. The midwives feared God more than Pharaoh. They refused to do what Pharaoh commanded them to do. God allowed the Israelites to be fruitful and multiply, just as He had promised Abraham.

Success for us may not take over four hundred years, but it will take time. We're not going to get everything right the first time. But we have to continue to allow God to grow us. When we plant and we don't see growth immediately, we may think we've failed. Give it time. Continue to cultivate what you've planted. In the parable of the barren fig tree, the owner of the vineyard looks for fruit on a fig tree for three years and doesn't find any. He tells the caretaker to cut it down. He doesn't want this fruitless tree using up the soil. The caretaker admonishes the owner to allow him one more year to dig around it and fertilize it. If the tree doesn't bear fruit then, he can cut it down (Lk. 13:6- 8). This is given as an illustration of giving people an opportunity to repent, but it is useful for us to remember when talking about success. We have to stay faithful to what God commissions us to do despite not seeing the growth or impact it will have right away. Don't give up before you have a chance to be successful.

Lambs, Rams, and Bushes

The second principle of success is **success requires sacrifice.** True success will require us to sacrifice. It may even call upon us to sacrifice the thing we see as growth or progress. God commands Abraham to sacrifice Isaac as a burnt offering (Gen. 22:2). God told Abraham he was going to be blessed with innumerable offspring. So far, God only gave him one son. Instead of giving him more sons and increasing him, God asks Abraham to sacrifice what he has. Abraham doesn't know how this is going to turn out, but he's still willing to trust God and give back what God gave him.

When we are successful and feel like we're on the right path, a threat to our success may cause us to close our fist and try to hold on to what little we have. This is not what gets blessed. What gets blessed is Abraham's willingness to do what God told him to do even when he didn't understand it in the moment. He is convinced God will provide and come through for him, and God does. God rewards Abraham's obedience by providing the sacrifice. Isn't it amazing how God gives us something to sacrifice? God gave Abraham Isaac, provided a ram to be sacrifice instead of Isaac, and blessed Abraham for his obedience.

Most of us believe we are struggling or being punished when things are being removed from our lives. We start to look for things we can change. We may keep adding people or things in an effort to enrich our lives. But what if things are being taken away so you can focus on God instead of having your affections divided? What if God is trying to show you whether or not you really trust Him with your life?

The Purge

The third principle of success is continuing to grow requires purging. Jesus tells His disciples in John 15 every branch bearing fruit is repeatedly pruned so it can bear more fruit (v. 2 AMP). Pruning is the strategic removal of parts of a plant to direct or control growth, improve or maintain health, harvest, or increase the yield of flowers and fruits. By cutting off one part, the whole is better able to grow.

Even though the Israelite experience outrageous growth in Egypt, a lot of this growth did not make it past a certain part of the journey. Of the 600,000 men who left Egypt (Ex. 12:37), only 2 made it into the Promised Land (Num. 14:29-30). Jesus says in John 15 the unproductive branches will be cut off and cast into the fire. God cuts off the unproductive parts. He is serious about growth, Sister.

We bring a lot of personal growth, personality and habits into our relationship with God. Some of those things will die during this journey. God will strip us of any part not producing fruit to ensure we continue to grow and yield an even bigger crop. Our success requires we get rid of any sin or weight weighing us down. God is directing and controlling our growth by removing what He knows   needs to go. Don't shy away from His shears.

Recalculating Route

The fourth principle of success is the **most direct route isn't always the best route.** If you have a Global Positioning System, or GPS, you may have noticed you are often given three different routes: the most direct, the quickest, and the cheapest. You can decide if avoiding tolls is more important to you than getting to your destination at a certain time. Taking the most direct route doesn't always guarantee you will be on time. Traffic and construction can hamper us all.

God did not take the Israelites by the most direct route. God had a good reason for taking them the long way around. These people had never been to battle and didn't know anything about fighting. They weren't conditioned. He knew if they met any opposition, they were going to fold. By taking the long way through the wilderness, God gives them time to develop. He prunes them little by little where they are before He moves them forward.

Maybe the route you are traveling has veered off from the most direct route to success. Others who started before you seem farther along than you are. People are questioning your pace. Do you really want to get there? Are you trying your best to get there? Why didn't you go this way? If you are following God's route for your life, arriving at your destination is guaranteed. Don't let people pull you off course with their directions; be led by the Lord.

How Does Your Garden Grow?

We must appreciate God's vision of success to continue to grow with Him. We have to appreciate the wilderness times of our lives. God isolates us and cuts us off from the world in a space where we can be developed and learn to replace the things of the world, the things of the flesh, with higher things, the things of the spirit.

This process looks ugly because it involves uprooting and digging out sin by the root. It's not comfortable. It feels like failure. But God is showing us areas where we are still weak, where we still struggle, where we still need Him. He's showing these areas to us in a contained environment where He can instruct us, not out in the open.

This reminds me of passages of scripture such as in Job 1 or in Isaiah 5 referring to a hedge God has around His people. Job 1 talks about the hedge of protection God has around Job to prevent certain things from happening to Him. The devil has to have permission to gain access to Job. God sets the parameters for what the devil can and can't do to Job. God doesn't allow anything into our lives without a reason. Successful people seek to find God's will in any circumstance.

In Isaiah 5, God talks about the vineyard He created, the children of Israel. He carefully cultivated this vineyard. He took all the rocks out and tilled the ground. God was planted, watered, and made sure the plants were protected from the elements to grow a good crop.

This is a great illustration of what the wilderness was. He took them out of where they were. He placed a hedge of protection around them. He removed all the things that could affect their growth. He planted them in good ground. Yet they still went wild and weren't suitable.

God took away His protection and left the Israelites exposed to the elements.

The last success principle I will give you is this: **whatever God cultivates will grow**. It doesn't matter how a situation appears to us. The correct result will be achieved with God. The only way we need to help God is by being obedient to what He tells us to do. Don't be wild grapes in the vineyard. Don't be an unproductive branch. Let's have the perspective of David and let goodness and mercy chase us down instead of chasing our idea of success.

CHAPTER EIGHTEEN

Holding on to Your Harvest

> ⁷Be not deceived; God is not mocked: for whatsoever a man soweth, that shall he also reap. ⁸For he that soweth to his flesh shall of the flesh reap corruption; but he that soweth to the Spirit shall of the Spirit reap life everlasting. ⁹And let us not be weary in well doing: for in due season we shall reap, if we faint not. ¹⁰As we have therefore opportunity, let us do good unto all men, especially unto them who are of the household of faith. Gal. 6:7-10

One of the most misunderstood concepts in the bible is the principle of sowing and reaping. On the surface, it seems simple: you will reap what you sow. In the larger Christian culture, this concept seems to be turned on its head. In an age of countless posts telling me to like, share, or type "amen" for this blessing I'm about to receive, it can be difficult for us as Christian women to understand the true nature of reaping a harvest.

After you've put in all the effort to take your walk with Christ seriously, after you have sown seeds of faithfulness, study, trust, and obedience, you expect to harvest the more abundant life Christ promised. The law of sowing and reaping, or the assurance you will reap what you sow, says you will receive it. You've survived the crows, the thorns, and the harsh heat of tribulation. You've cultivated and cared for the fragile plant of faith, and now there's fruit on your tree. It's harvest time.

I would be remiss if I didn't insert a bit of caution here. What I have found in my times of plenty—when I have enjoyed a full crop of spiritual, mental, emotional, physical, or material blessings—is no matter how much I have, it's hard to hold on to. It slips through my fingers. Sometimes it's so gradual I barely notice until it's almost gone. Even though I've done the work and should be enjoying the fruits of my labor, I often find myself...fruitless in a surprisingly short amount of time.

Maybe this happens to you: you get more than you expected, but somehow you find yourself with less than you anticipated. You get what you've been praying earnestly for, but the happiness wears off in a matter of hours, if not minutes. It's not a matter of being ungrateful or irresponsible; you are diligent in thanking God and you attempt to use the things you earn effectively. But somehow, all the things you worked so hard for are used up so quickly.

I want to tell you your breakthrough is coming. I want to say God is about to open up the windows of Heaven and pour out a bigger blessing than you can hold. I would love to tell you God is going to bless you with more than enough to take care of your every need and want, and all you have to do is shout glory to God every now and then to maintain it. After all, I've spent all of this time making you examine yourself and do the hard work; now should be the reward, right?

But it doesn't work this way. We can't sit down at the end of all this work and enjoy the fruits of our labor without more work. The thing people never want to tell you about harvest time is how much work is required. Any farmer can tell you harvest time requires more help in the fields. The hours are longer, the work more strenuous. You have to be just as dedicated to harvest as you were when you were sowing.

If you want to see prime examples of the work required at harvest time, you will find a few depictions in the bible. The story of Ruth takes place during harvest time. Ruth goes behind the reapers in the field and gleans what they leave behind for the poor and foreigners per the Law of Moses (Lev. 23:22, Deut. 24:19). They were intentional about leaving something for others. This is a good principle to keep in mind when we harvest.

Not only do the laborers gather the crop, but they thresh it as well. Threshing, also known is sifting or winnowing, is a process by which the loose outer part of the grain is separated from the grain. It is the process by which wheat is separated from the chaff. Jesus describes the devil as asking to have Peter, to sift him as wheat (Luke 22:31). In this Christ says He has prayed for Peter's faith not to fail. In other words, we will have to separate the chaff from the wheat at harvest time. The useless bits will blow away on the wind in the sifting process.

Another example of harvesting can be found in the story of Joseph (Gen. 41). The king of Egypt has a dream and Joseph interprets it. There will be seven years of plenty and seven years of famine in the land. They must prepare for the seven years of famine by setting a fifth of their harvests aside during the seven years of plenty. When the famine hits, Joseph opens up the storehouses and gives grain to the people of Egypt. He has so much in store he is able to sell to others.

A principle of harvesting we can take away from this is not to use everything we get. We must lay something aside or in store for the time to come. Unlike Joseph, we don't know what is on the morrow (Jas. 4:14). It is always better to be prepared than to pay the penalty for lack of prudence.

Help Wanted

> The harvest is plenteous, but the laborers are few.
> Matt. 9:37; Lk. 10:2

No matter what season of life we are in, we should be reapers. The fields of this world are white with a harvest for the Lord. Many have planted and watered and the increase is staring us in the face. Jesus is looking for workers who will reap this harvest. But will you be a worker for the Lord? I've seen a marked shift in my generation away from working at an established company. Everyone wants to have their own business or brand. No one wants to spend their time working on someone else's dream. Everyone wants to be the boss and control their income. No one wants to punch a clock or be accountable to anyone.

While this may be a positive in the business world, this perspective does us a disservice as subjects in the kingdom of God. A king can enlist his subjects to perform whatever job he deems necessary in the kingdom. God, our king, has work for us to do. He didn't give us everything we have to please ourselves. He gave it to us to work for Him. If we don't use what He gave us for His glory, what we have will be taken away from us.

The fact of the matter is we all work for someone. Those who the devil uses for his purposes, those who "work" for sin, receive a wage of death. I don't know about you, but I work too hard to be paid death for my work. Sin doesn't pay as well as God does. The benefits of serving sin don't compare with the benefits of serving God.

God is not mocked, Sisters: we will reap what we have sown. When harvest time comes, what will you be reaping? What has grown in the field of your heart? What did you plant in your heart? What did you cultivate and feed? What is left the locusts or crows haven't eaten? Can you, like Joseph, open up the storehouses and mete out the fruit of your labor to others who have need? Or are you in line to receive from another?

In order to hold on to a harvest, you have to have one. In order to reap, you have to sow. You have to cultivate what you have sown. The plant must be nurtured by the rains and the heat of the sun to grow to its full potential. You have to do the work to reap the reward.

The other way to reap is to work for the Lord. The Lord's fields are ready to be harvested right now. You can be a reaper for the Lord while a crop is growing in your life. You don't need to sit and watch it grow. Instead, focus on the fields ripe for harvesting. Save souls. Encourage and exhort your sisters and brothers. Work diligently onto the Lord. This will yield your true harvest.

How do you hold on to your harvest? How do you "lay up for yourselves treasure in heaven, where neither moth nor rust doth corrupt, and where thieves do not break through nor steal (Matt. 6:20)"?

1. **Recognize where the increase comes from.** The world would have you to believe if you hustle harder, work harder, and give more of your time, energy, and effort to your pursuits, you will yield more. However, this model is proven false every day. A crop you worked hard to cultivate can be eaten by crows or locusts. You can be the best real estate there is and the housing bubble can burst just as you reach the top. You can die of overwork before you reap the rewards of your labor. Time and chance happens to us all. But the bible teaches us a different way than going into a city, buying, selling and getting gain. We can have knowledge of when and what to plant, how much to water, and how much sunlight and plant needs. We can even plant and water. But God gives the increase. There are you'll plant and never see grow. There are plants you don't plant or water but will benefit from their increase. Whatever God's will is for your life will grow. Keeping this in the proper perspective is essential for holding on to your harvest. If you know the source, you can go back to it when you need more. You have an understanding of who it really belongs to. You will focus more of your attention on being a good steward of what you have been given than on the addiction of acquisition.
2. **Be mindful of who you're giving your time, energy, effort, and money.** The Bible tell us not to owe any man anything. It also tells us some harsh truths about being lenders and what we are responsible for when we choose to lend to people.

Helping people is not something we are always supposed to do. That's a hard one for us to swallow because we have family members or others we want to help. However, we have to be wary of people who drain us of all our resources. They don't put anything back into us. They deplete us. We have to have discernment with what we choose to give our time, energy or money. This includes people and relationships. You want to be able to give God the first fruits of everything you have. You want to have enough left over to sustain you through times when you are unable to grow or gather. You'll need to be sustained by what you have reaped. If you give it all away, at some point before there is anything else coming in, you're going to be without. Being able to say "no" to people is essential to holding on to your harvest. Learn how to offer alternatives to people and encourage people to take care of themselves and take heed to themselves.

3. **Know when to pull away and be with the Father.** Jesus did this several times during His ministry. We must know how to hold back some of our time, energy, money and effort. We shouldn't expend all of our resources on people, the pursuit of material gain, or recognition. It can't be all about grinding for success in the business arena, getting more money, and having more friends in order to be what this world deems to be successful.

4. **There should be restrictions in place to govern how we utilize the harvest we've been given to make it last as long as we need it.** We shouldn't become stingy, but we should be a good steward of the things God has given us.

5. **Stop competing on the world's terms.** When we are comparing ourselves to other women, we may subconsciously see ourselves in competition with them. We can waste a lot of time, energy, and

money chasing an ideal or trying to live up to an impossible standard of beauty or brilliance. God doesn't call us to chase worldly standards of perfection; He calls us to get our definitions of success and perfection from Him. Not only are we not called to this pursuit, it doesn't serve us or the other woman. Holding her to a standard of perfection you created around what you know of her life keeps you from seeing areas of connection between you, ways in which you can help each other be better in Christ. Here's the truth we need to remember: whatever God wants to come to pass is going to come to pass no matter what we're trying to do. We need to be mindful of the fact the competition is rigged. Whoever God has selected for something is the one who will get it.

6. **Stewardship.** I've used the term "good steward" a number of times to describe the main idea behind holding on to your harvest. God has entrusted us with things. None of this is ours. If you want to make the most of what you have been given, then you have to realize it's not yours. We have to be open to using what God left us in charge of the way He wants us to use it.

CONCLUDING THOUGHTS

Choose Life

¹⁵See, I have set before thee this day life and good, and death and evil; ¹⁶In that I command thee this day to love the Lord thy God, to walk in his ways, and to keep his commandments and his statutes and his judgments, that thou mayest live and multiply: and the Lord they God shall bless thee in the land whither thou goest to possess it. ¹⁷But if thine heart turn away, so that thou wilt not hear, but shalt be drawn away, and worship other gods and serve them; ¹⁸I denounce unto you this day, that ye shall surely perish, and that ye shall not prolong your days upon the land, whither thou passest over Jordan to go to possess it. ¹⁹I call heaven and earth to record this day against you, that I have set before you life and death, blessing and cursing: therefore choose life, that both thou and thy seed may live. ²⁰That thou mayest love the Lord thy God, and that thou mayest obey his voice, and that thou mayest cleave unto him: for he is thy life, and the length of thy days: that thou mayest dwell in the land which the Lord sware unto thy fathers, to Abraham, to Isaac, and to Jacob, to give them.

Moses tells the Israelites behold I lay before you this day death and life; choose life. This is just as relevant for us today. We've already talked about choosing who you will serve in "A Woman in the Middle." We know what each side has to offer. It's decision time. Choose life, sister.

The content of this book can be overwhelming, but the message is simple: Choose ye this day whom you will serve. Each step of the way, through every topic I've covered, through every season we've put into perspective and tried to find ways to keep growing, the ultimate goal is just to choose. When are we choosing for? Today. Each and every day, while it is today. Choose to follow God today, dear sister. Decide in each moment you are faced with to choose Him again. I don't have ten foolproof steps for spiritual growth or being "Super-Christian." I'm not attempting to give you the Seven Habits of Highly Effective Christians. I can only give you what Paul gave me:

Forgetting those things that are behind I press on to the mark of the high calling in Jesus Christ.

I press for on toward the mark by choosing Him each day. I consider Him when making my decisions. I consult with Him on my life. I cling to the knowledge if I abide in Him, I will be fruitful, and apart from Him, I can do nothing.

I opened this book with a question. This entire book is the answer to the question, but this more than anything: choose life, sisters. The life Christ is. The life He gave. Lay down your life and pick up the life He laid down for you. You can't choose it for anyone else, past or present. You can't make anyone live in the light of this decision. But you make this decision, and you live it out.

Choose the Way, the Truth, and the Life.

About the Author

Erica Denise Hearns first began writing at the age of five with a story about a princess named Jasmine (which she insists was NOT based on the Disney fairytale). She was first published at the age of eight and has won numerous creative writing and oratory awards. She has published several poems and essays and even authored an advice column for the newsletter for the Horizons-Upward Bound program. She graduated with a B.A. in English from the University of Central Florida in 2008.

Erica was inspired to write her first book, *Altered before the Altar,* when she realized the teenage and young adult women she taught needed help putting dating, love and relationships into the proper perspective—and so did she. She has since published *Altered before the Altar: The Devotional Study Guide* and *A Serious Prayer Journal,* a 21 day prayer journal with prompts modeled after The Lord's Prayer. She lives and writes in Orlando, Florida.

www.ingramcontent.com/pod-product-compliance
Lightning Source LLC
Chambersburg PA
CBHW071312110426
42743CB00042B/1297